AF262823

PORTRAIT OF MY FATHER

Also by Jordan Stein

Rip Tales: Jay DeFeo's Estocada & Other Pieces
Miyoko Ito: Heart of Hearts

Stephen Kaltenbach

Portrait of My Father

by Jordan Stein

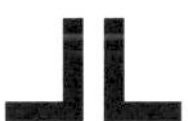

For Connie Lewallen (1939–2022)

A friend and teacher who introduced
me to Steve and much more.

CONTENTS

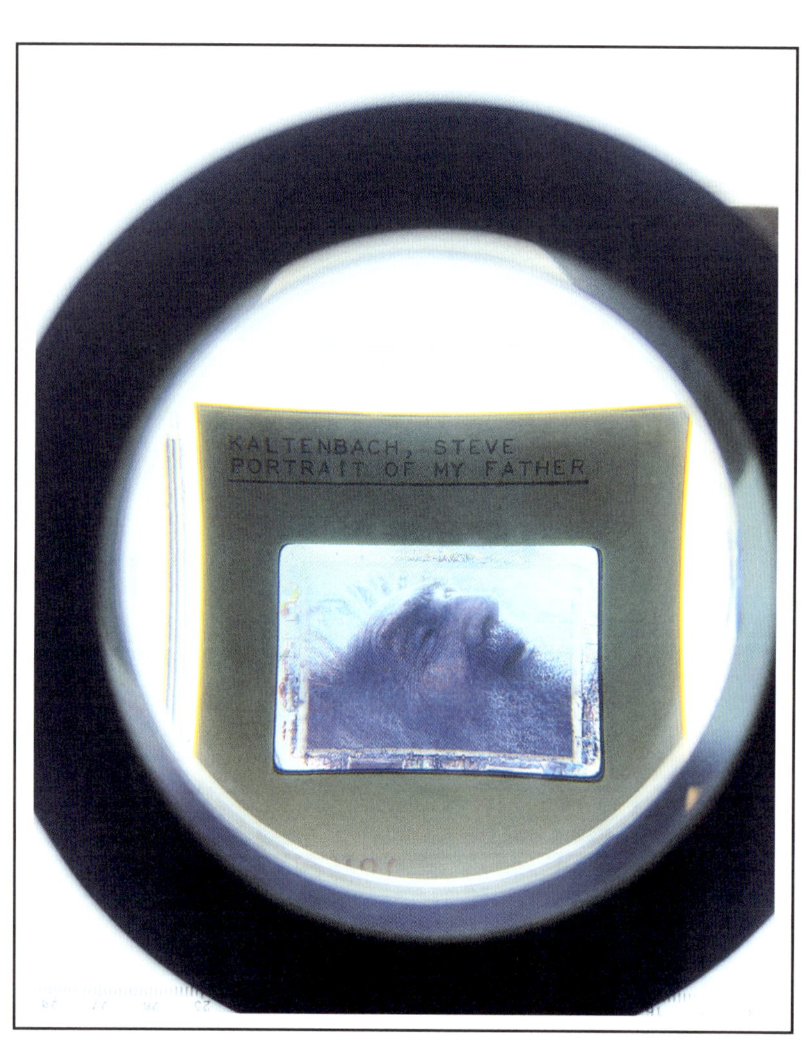
KALTENBACH, STEVE
PORTRAIT OF MY FATHER

INTRODUCTION

In 1972, the artist Stephen Kaltenbach began developing a monumental painting called *Portrait of My Father*. Sustained by a formidable love for his subject, experience with psychedelics, and a blooming spiritual life, he worked for nearly seven years to finish it — mainly from a rented barn in the Central Valley of California, where he lived without plumbing or insulation. The painting holds a significant place not only in the Crocker Art Museum in Sacramento, where it hangs on permanent display, but also in the imaginations of those who have experienced its peculiar and overwhelming presence in person.

Portrait of My Father is mind-boggling from across the room, a nearly 10-by-15-foot photorealistic depiction of a man on death's door, and from up close, as each trippy beard whisker explodes a window onto eternity. Intimate and epic, human and cosmic, it is beyond trend or school, a work of art in its own big, strange lane.

In the barn he was an outsider, but Kaltenbach had arrived from the leading edge of the New York art world. He had explored the potency and malleability of ideas during graduate school at the University of California, Davis, and in late 1960s SoHo embarked on several bodies of work that could pass for existential riddles, factoring time and context as critical ingredients in their reception. There were metal time capsules meant to be opened on the occasion of his death, anonymous advertisements placed in a leading art magazine, and ideas carefully planted in the minds of other artists, like seeds.

Wary of success and eager to push his contrarian impulses to their breaking point, a twenty-something Kaltenbach enacted an experiment he called the "Protocol of Opposites," a method of encouraging precisely what was least expected of him as an artist. In the process, he challenged several received orthodoxies of Conceptualism, the new and leading art milieu privileging ideas above all else, and scratched at the boundaries of the impossibly large ontological categories we commonly refer to as art and life.

In the first line of a 1970 *Artforum* interview, he says, "I think most of the work is heavily weighted towards ideas and away from the visual." So how did he physically, mentally, and spiritually get from city to country, arriving not just at the visual, but the visually colossal? And perhaps most significantly, how can *Portrait*'s undeniable earnestness coexist with the irony of its "Opposite" origins?

Portrait was made by an idea-based artist — a non-painter who put his mind to it, an artist who left New York in 1970 as an artwork in and of itself, as a commitment to the unexpected. It was painted by an artist who paid 25 dollars a month for a barn where he became both himself and somebody else, dropping so far out he emerged on the other side.

To make a life in art, to make a career, the itinerary — then as now — is clear: stay the dominant artistic and social course, meet the right people, show at the right places, and break the right rule or two. But for Kaltenbach, these conventions invited a series of rarely considered mirror questions that more broadly critiqued taste, class, and value: Where were the wrong places? Who were the wrong people? And which were the wrong exhibitions? Art history tends to disfavor the outliers, let alone the genre of what might be described as large-scale psychedelic portraiture. For better and for worse, a meaningful percentage of Kaltenbach's life was committed to a canvas likely to be out of fashion in most conceivable eras.

That such a noteworthy painting is underknown outside of California's Central Valley is predictable and lamentable, a consequence of countless works of art unfairly maligned as regional and of the artist's decision to abandon a traditional path and cadre of ostensibly like-minded peers in the global art capital of New York. For those on the make, disappearance is death. But for others, there is vitality that only a certain type of retreat affords — one that trades visibility for the conditions of self-discovery and swaps well-worn narratives of success and failure for a more varied unpredictability. To the scene Kaltenbach abandoned, *Portrait of My Father* was beyond heretical in its style, form, content, medium, and more. And to think that it was nearly a portrait of his cat, a Persian longhair named Teddy.

In the early days of the pandemic, I reached out to learn more about the painting and its maker. I was writing a book centered on Jay DeFeo, another California artist who worked for roughly the same number of years on a single painting called *The Rose* (1958–1966). I never had the chance to meet DeFeo (she died in 1989), but here was Kaltenbach, living and working in Davis, just an hour and a half northwest of my home in San Francisco. Why not pick up the phone?

I proposed that I perform the definitive *Portrait* interview; he agreed, on the condition that I present him with an outline beforehand. My first question invited him to address the circumstances surrounding his move from New York, where I'd heard he was dating the brilliant and uncompromising artist Lee Lozano (which turned out to be false), to Sacramento, where he was to teach at California State University, Sacramento, known informally as Sacramento State.

Two hours in, we were still thousands of miles from the barn.

Over the next week or so we recorded nearly ten hours of conversation. For a time, I thought we might never arrive at *Portrait*. I also suspected that his masterpiece might be the most difficult object in his orbit to talk about; it seemed that in the barn, the painting *was* his life, a portrait not just of his father, but the psychedelic latticework of the artist's consciousness. I feared he might contend that *Portrait of My Father* is quite beyond words, so why bother discussing it? But, finally, he did discuss it, and much more, in vivid and compelling detail.

Steve can speak elliptically, and the pace and content of our dialogue varied from day to day. Additionally, secrets and lies are useful tools not only in his art practice, but in the way he relates his past. "Tell a lie" and "Perpetrate a hoax" literally appear across the face of certain artworks, and the artist has intentionally redacted and backdated works, changed titles, and invented pieces through storytelling, dropping them into dialogue with those in a position to contribute to the construction of art history. He's even suggested that everything since leaving New York, above and beyond the making of *Portrait*, was a conscious effort to become a "regional artist," subverting or at least complicating the painting's sincerity.

Perhaps he is in line with fiction writers, exploring the power of lies in the service of truth. It may also be accurate to say that in addition to metal and paint, Kaltenbach's chosen media include unreliability, memory loss, and bullshit. If the past is defined by its perpetual disappearance, and history is written by the winners, why not be an overactive participant in the reconstruction and deconstruction of one's own CV?

Over the course of our dialogue, I occasionally had the feeling he was putting me on, telling tall tales atop an already soaring mountaintop. Other times, and more prosaically, his chronology simply didn't even out. And yet, while many of his pronouncements can't exactly be disproven, the sheer thingness of *Portrait of My Father* is indisputable. It *is*, whether or not his many stories surrounding the immense artwork are exactly true.

What began as my interest in chronicling the construction of a single painting transformed into a kind of selected and improvisatory autobiography narrated by Stephen Kaltenbach. I didn't aim to redirect the artist, and it eventually became clear that the sweeping contours of his life and mind greatly informed my understanding of his *Portrait*, particularly as I began editing and then annotating our conversations.

From his pastoral childhood to graduate school alongside Bruce Nauman, and from his arrival in SoHo to his defiant departure, his story came to feel far greater than the sum of its parts. That said, I still have questions — questions about the line between art and life, and about the transformation of a person and a painting that defy so many of my expectations.

It's challenging to move both toward and away from something in equal measure, and very hard to know at what ratio the artist's turn from received social and cultural norms coexisted with his artistic and religious awakening. In some ways, this is the central question of both the painting and Kaltenbach's adult life. It's fitting, then, that he and his art sometimes give opposing answers.

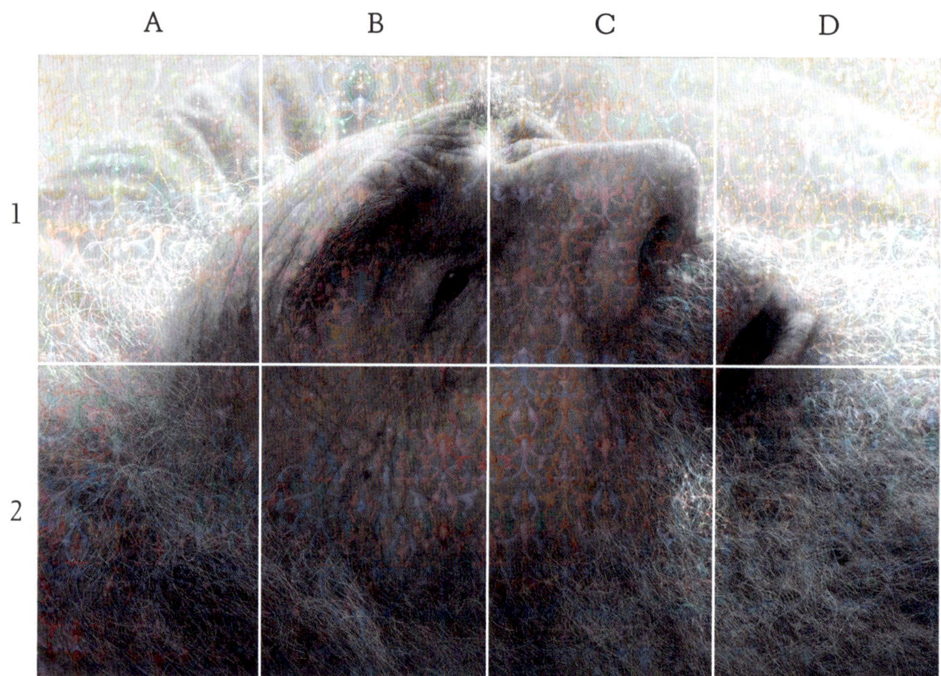

Key to the following pages.

PORTRAIT OF MY FATHER

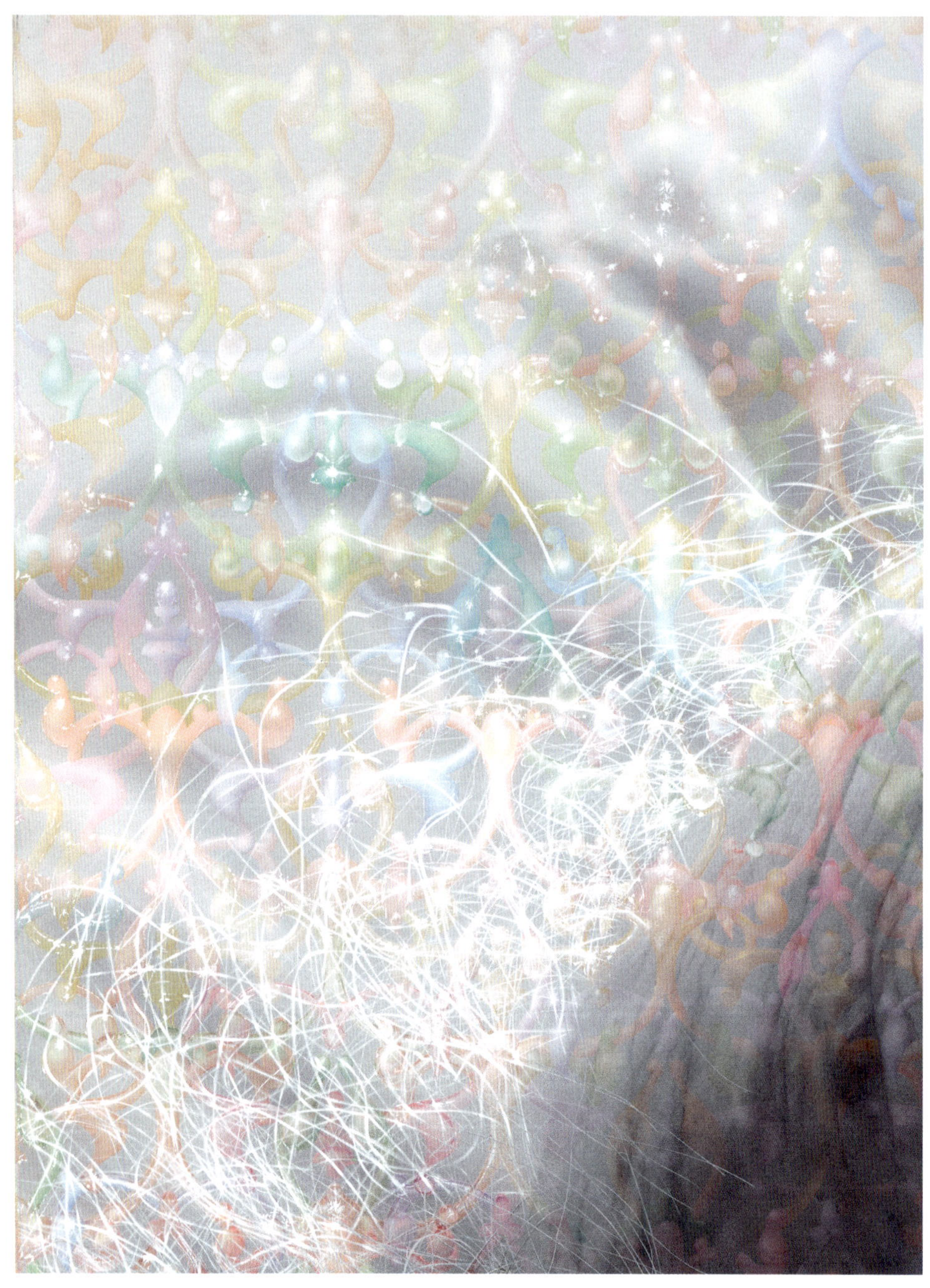

A-1

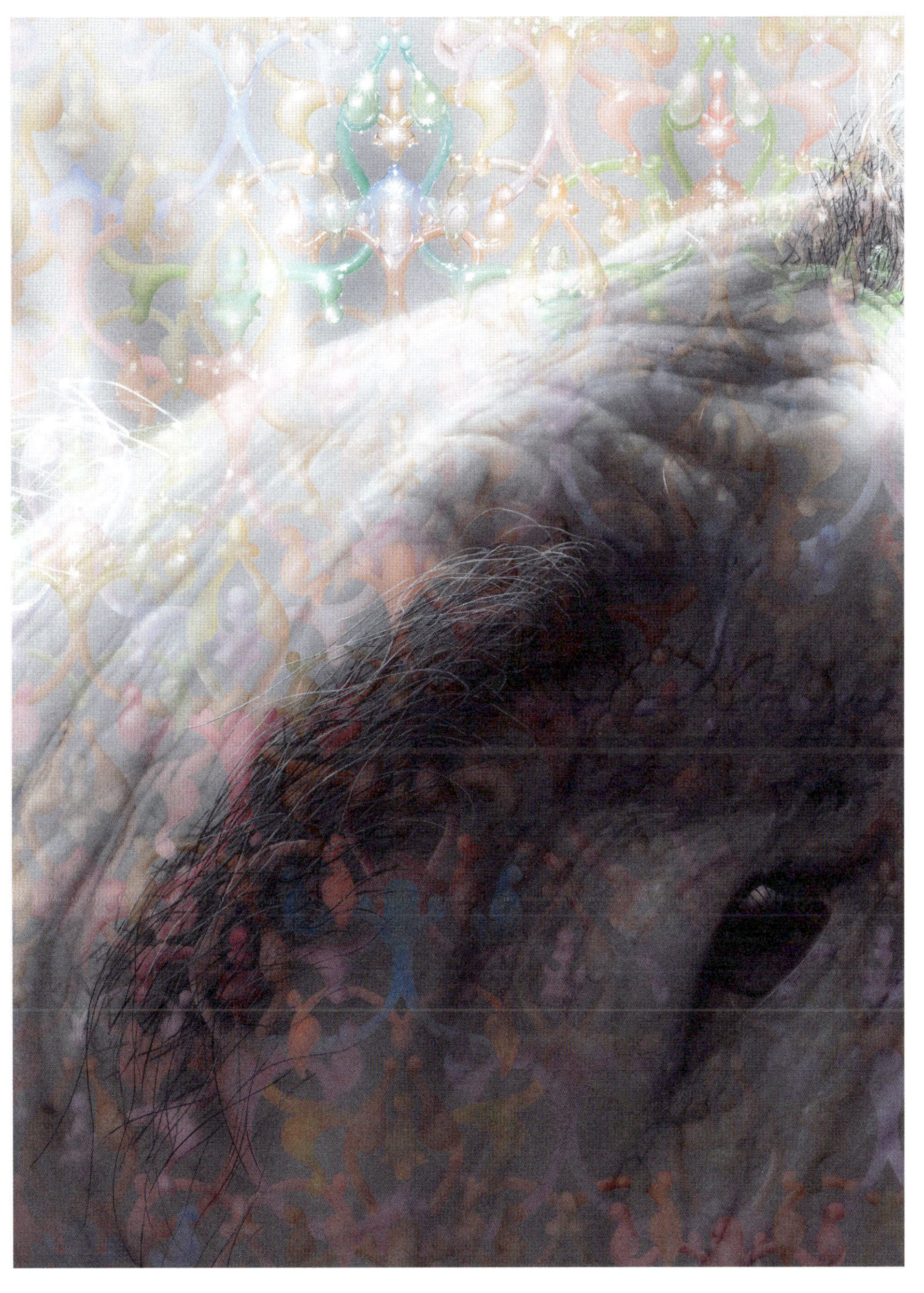

B-1

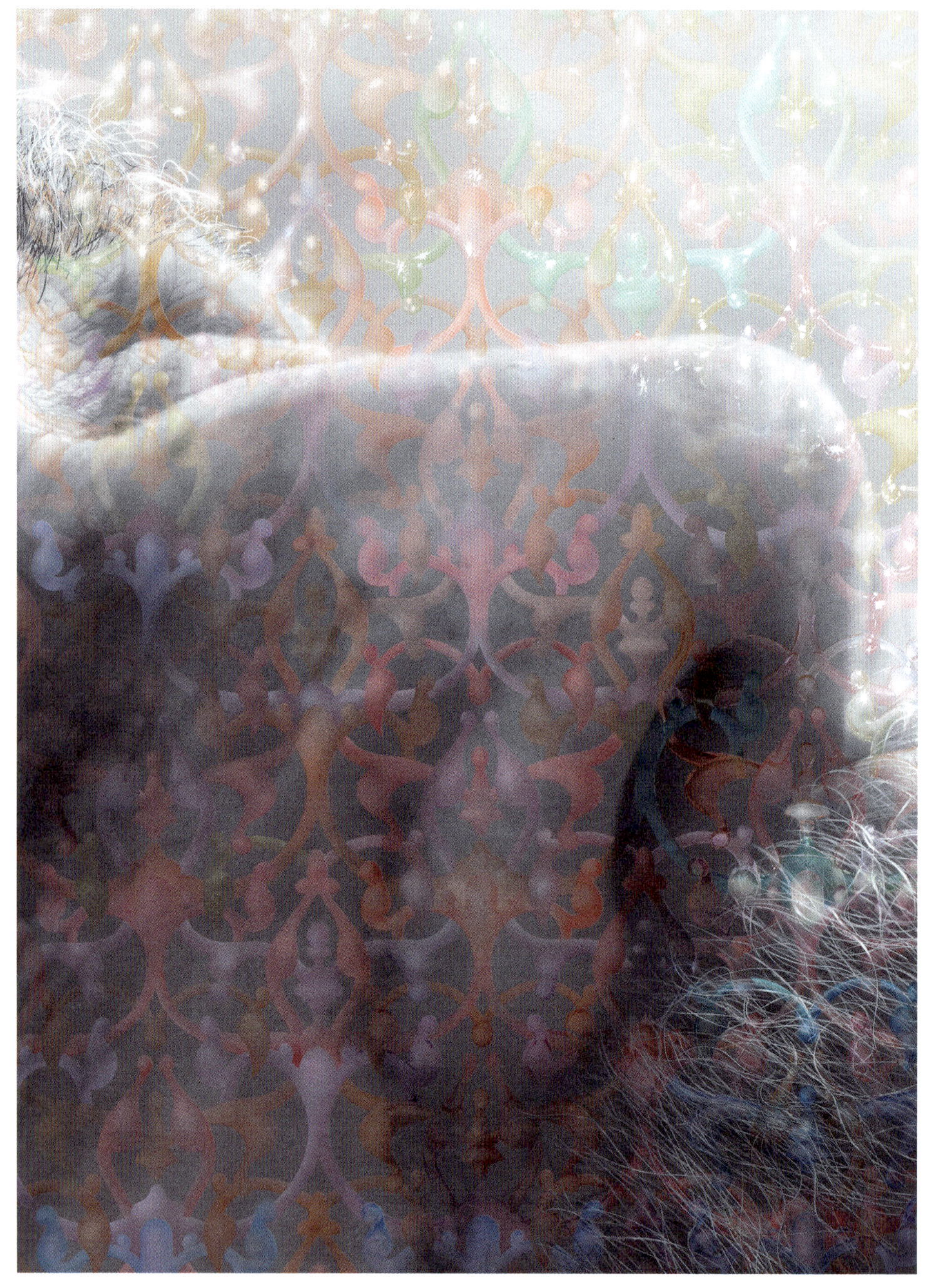

C-1

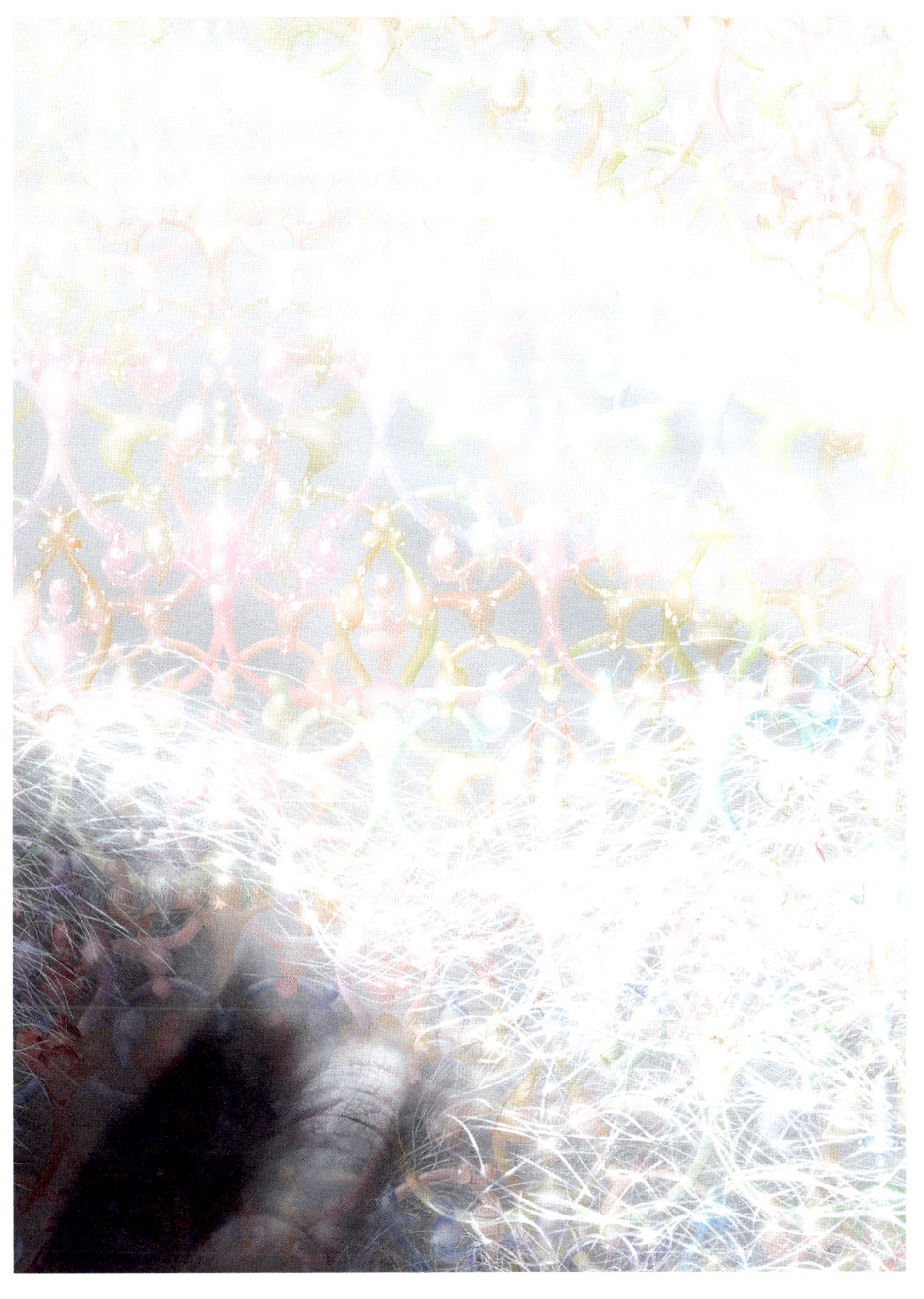

D-1

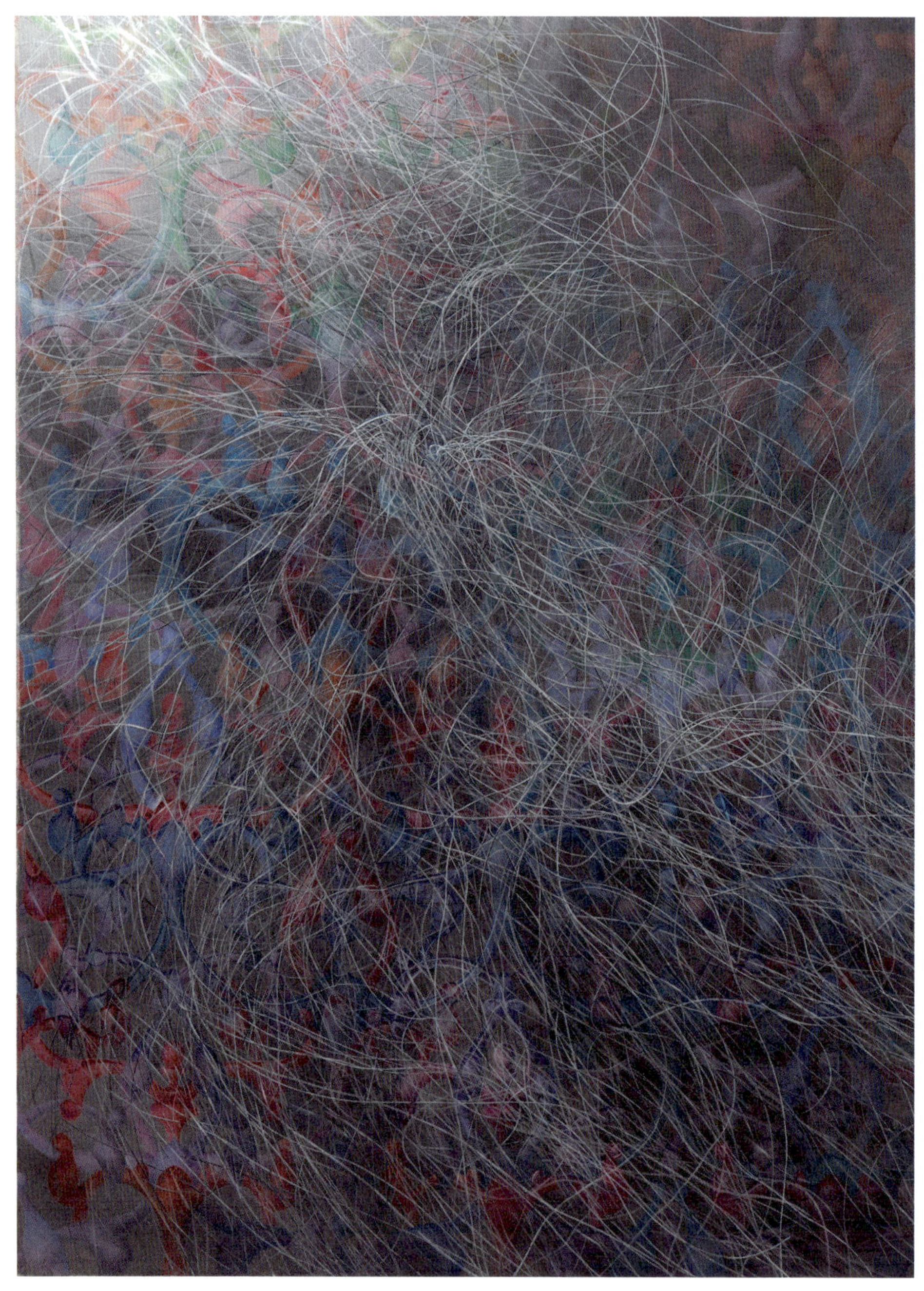

A-2

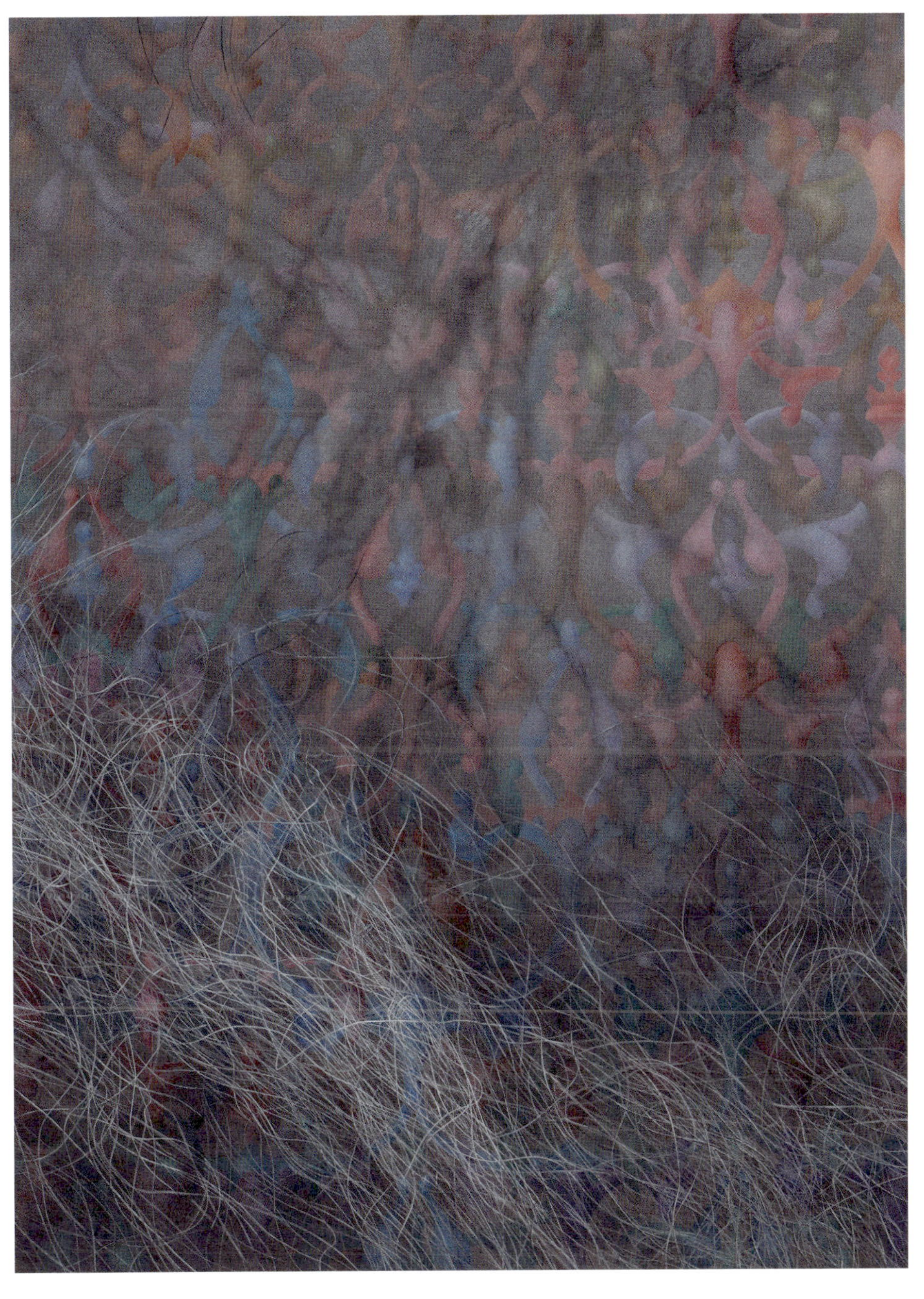

B-2

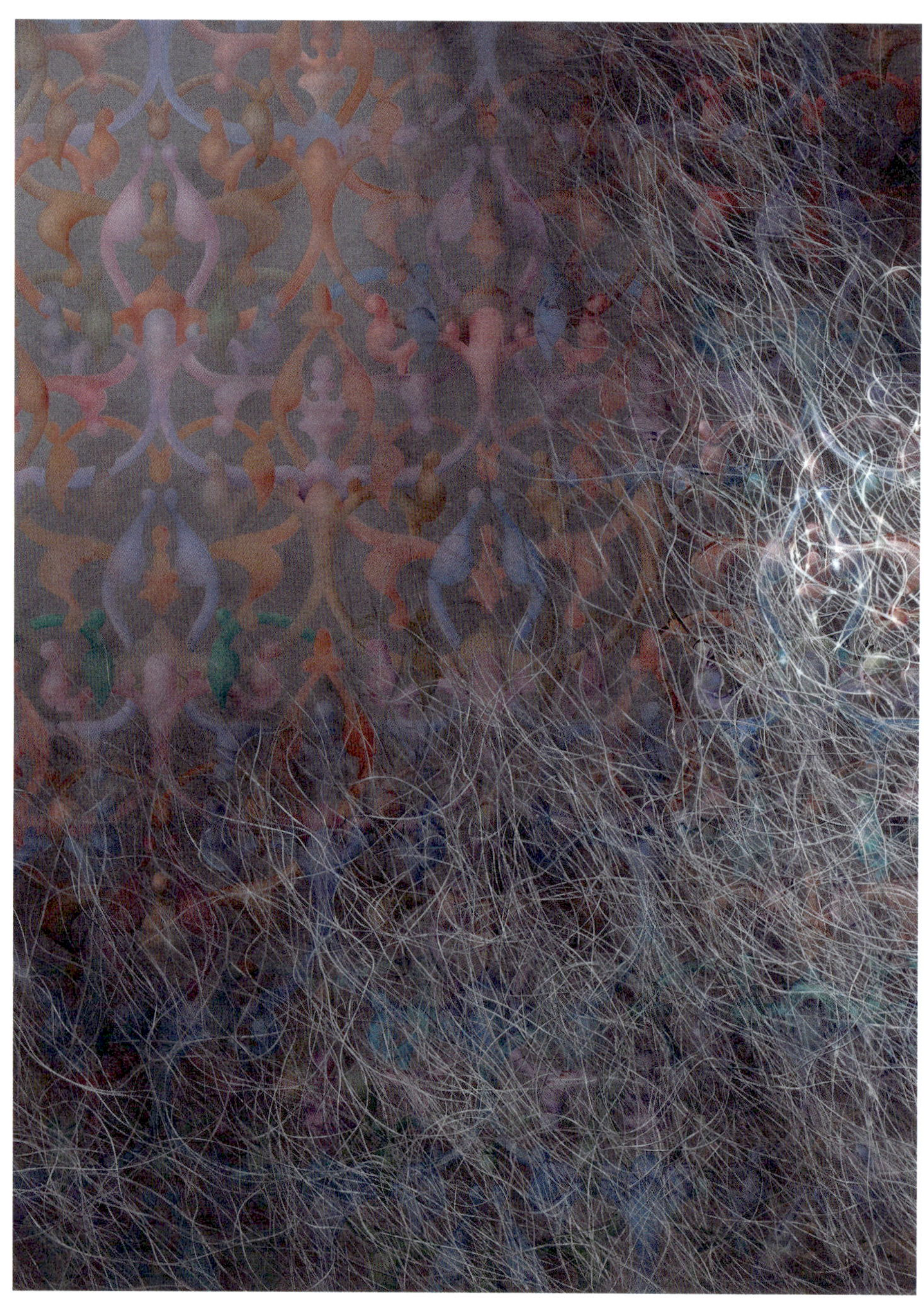

C-2

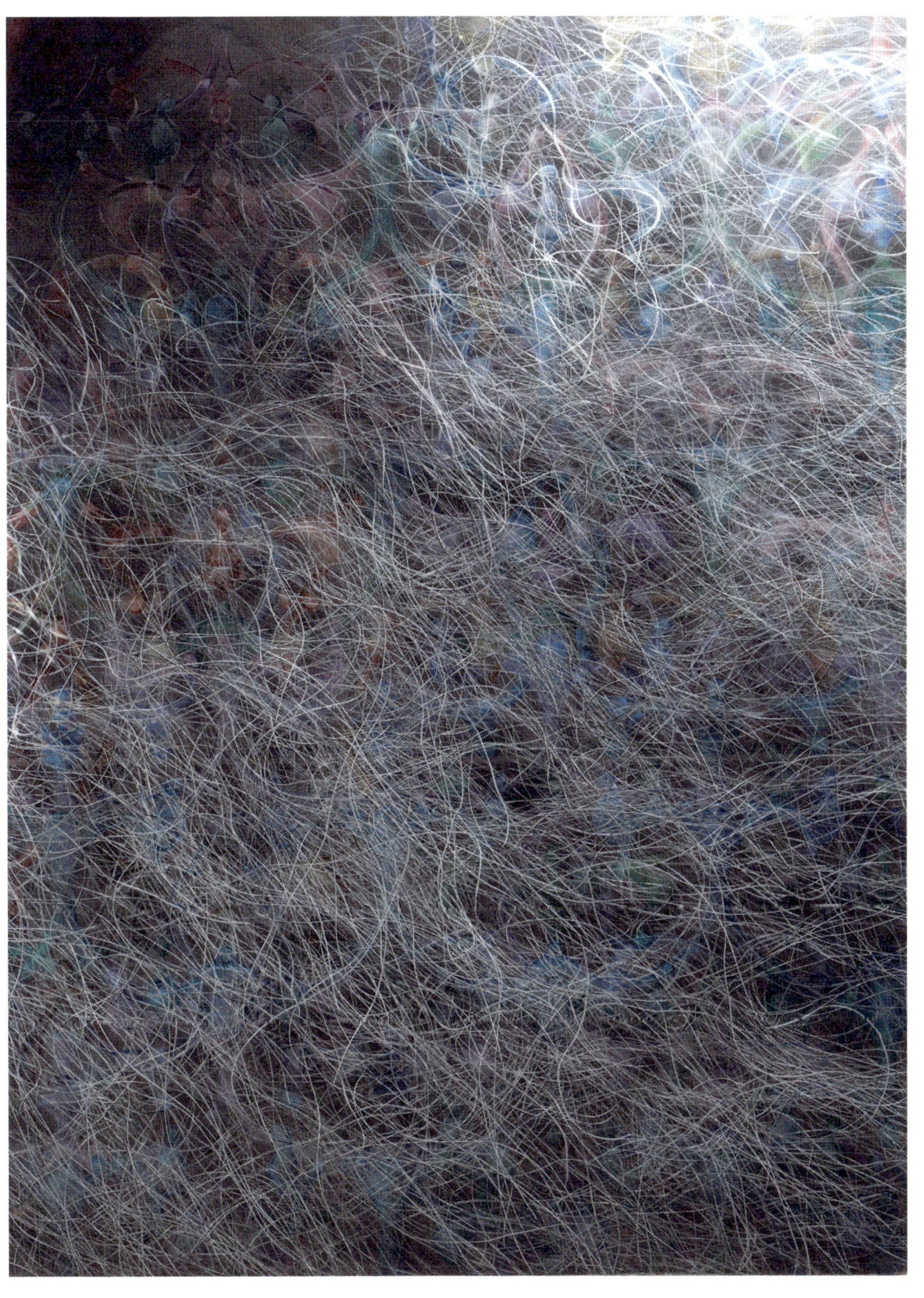

D-2

A note on the typesetting — The backbone of this publication is a dialogue between Jordan Stein and Stephen Kaltenbach; it is set on the left margin, and speaking voices are indicated by initials. Stein's annotations, which occasionally include quotations from other sources, appear indented and italicized.

SK: I took my first psychedelic trip in the spring semester of 1968. I became friends with two of my students at the School of Visual Arts, Peter and Eric; I invited them over for dinner one night. They both seemed to be more perceptive than I'd experienced them in class, and I said some kind of smart-ass remark like, "Do you guys leave your IQs at home when you come to school?"

"We took this drug before we came over," they told me.

"What drug?"

"Mescaline," they said.

"Is that like LSD, and if it is, how can you be sitting here eating dinner?" From what I knew, it seemed like something you wouldn't want to take over dinner.

"Oh no, it just makes things clearer."

I told them that sounded like a great idea.

"Well, we brought you some." And they gave me a couple of capsules, gel caps.

As soon as they left, I got a glass of water to take them, and there's a knock on my door. It was my upstairs neighbor, a very good painter, John Torreano; he lived on the fourth floor, and I lived on the second. He knocked on the door and asked what I was doing. I said, "Funny you should ask. I'm about to take this new drug." Of course, it wasn't a new drug, but it was new to me.

"Oh, that sounds good. ... Do you have any extra?"

"Well, I have two right here!"

I gave him one, luckily, because a half-hour later my reality had become so abstract that I felt I couldn't really respond to what was happening in my mind, conceptually and experientially. I think that being alone could have been a little freaky, especially if I was twice as far gone. The experience became so visually entertaining that it didn't matter that my mind was working in ways that were

— to some degree — disconcerting, because I saw amazing patterning that overlapped and filled the air, filled the solids, and, most strangely, did not conflict with other things in my field of vision.

I remember going upstairs to look at John's paintings and the patterning I was seeing harmonized perfectly with them. Interestingly enough, he had a number of completed works leaning against the wall, facing away from the room, and the backs looked as good as the fronts. It just didn't matter. I think I realized that this vision was not going to go away, and I never forgot it.

What I wanted to do with painting was to reproduce my psychedelic experience as much as possible, and to deeply investigate the pattern/image combination. I wanted to get as far into that as I could and see how it worked and what it would do.

The problem with painting two images on the same surface is being able to portray both without conflict between them; if either is too strong, neither will work. My assignment was to reduce that conflict as much as possible while allowing for a certain kind of dimensionality that's hard to explain; it's something that went along with the visions that John and I had on mescaline. There was an exultation of spirit that we both felt was very strongly connected with our visual experience.

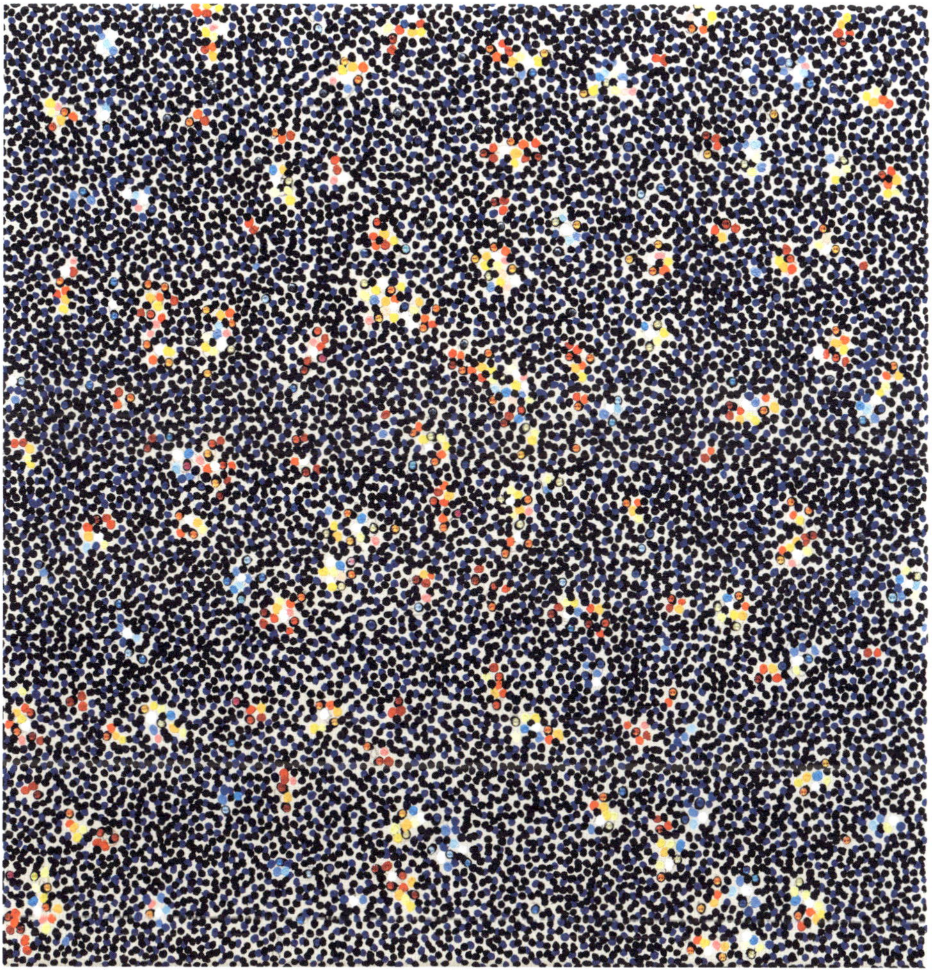

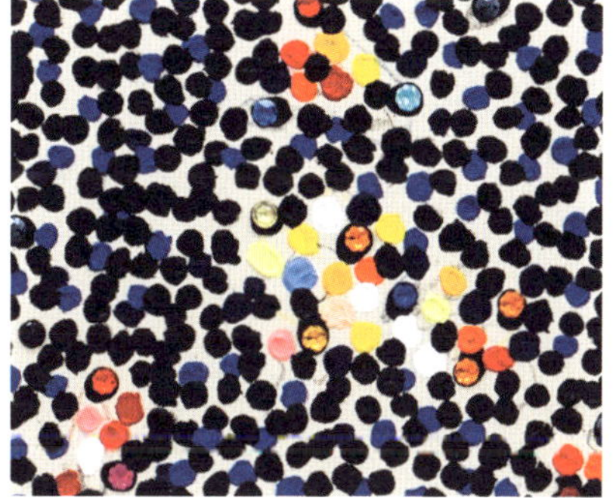

John Torreano, *Galaxie*, 1979
Acrylic gems and acrylic paint on
canvas, 72 × 72 inches (plus detail),
Image courtesy Thomas Brambilla
Gallery © John Torreano

SK: I drove to California every summer when I lived in New York to avoid the humidity; I also didn't have a job in New York during the summers. I was still friends with people at UC Davis, so I was able to teach summer classes there.

In the summer of 1968, I was driving out and the car was destroyed. Actually, my student was driving. I was taking photographs, and we ran into a hailstorm — we were following the terrific clouds. I'd never seen anything like it. We decided to retrace our path, go back about 10 miles and through the town of Taos, the artist colony in New Mexico. I thought, well, we can see that, and I can photograph these clouds. We're driving along. All of a sudden, this chunk of ice bounced off the hood and left a big dent. It was a brand-new Mercedes-Benz that I was driving to LA for a car delivery service, and it was owned by the actor Richard Boone, who played Paladin the gunslinger on the TV show *Have Gun – Will Travel*.

How am I going to explain this dent in the hood? Then another piece of hail hit, then 50, and then 1,000. It was like being in a snare drum. I had my girlfriend, two students, and our two cats in the car, and it was just really loud. Then the windshield in the back window broke, and it knocked the hood ornament off and broke a headlight. The car was thoroughly battered. We stopped in Taos and called the guy in Los Angeles and told him his car was destroyed.

I used the photographs to paint *Sunset*, and I was hoping that I could come to understand enough about painting to actually make it. I didn't have a clear idea of what to do until I visited Malcolm Morley's studio. We worked together at the School of Visual Arts. He's a funny guy, and I liked his painting.

I went over, and I was looking at a painting in his studio, and I was pretty amazed that you couldn't tell where he stopped one day and started again the next day. There were no ghosts. I remember thinking, *How did he do that? There's no way that the painting was done square by square.*

The "ghosts" Kaltenbach is describing are grid lines used by artists to map an image — in this case a photograph — square by square onto the surface of a canvas.

Then I saw in my mind how a painting would look if there were ghost grid patterns. It just all of a sudden hit me. I thought, *That's how I can make this painting.* I went home super-excited — I remember thinking I can change the value from one square to the next. I can change the hue, I can change the tint, tone. Anything you can describe, I could shift between each segment.

He would embrace the discrepancies instead of laboring over their elimination.

So I put a fish-scale pattern over the photograph and had that silk-screened on a painting panel. Then I just copied from the photograph to the panel, depending on where it was in the photograph — if it was over the sun, it was pure white; if it was over the cloud, it was that version of gray or blue or whatever. It reproduced bigger in oil paint. And then I varied the color a little bit, so when you stood back and looked, there was a flickery thing. It took three months. I remember having to go back to the beginning and repaint the first 10 percent because it was a little bit sketchy.

> Sunset *depicts a dramatic cloudscape over a series of mountain ridges at the bottom edge of the canvas. The sun is largely hidden by clouds, bursting forth in rays. Light and dark shades of blue, orange, and purple dominate. The landscape is covered with a repeating pattern of interlocking ovals with curved diamond-shape interiors that resembles chain link; the form both complements and sits apart from the landscape. Despite its origin story, the tone is tranquil.*

SK: I did a whole series of pattern collages as research and ended up having a show at Reese Palley of the *Sunset* painting and some space collages.

> *Kaltenbach showed* Sunset *in 1972 at the short-lived Reese Palley Gallery in San Francisco, named for its eccentric founder, an Atlantic City-born entrepreneur, nuclear-power expert, global-warming crusader, Torah smuggler, and art dealer. Palley initially leased Frank Lloyd Wright's only San Francisco building to sell elaborate porcelain birds, but hired a young curator named Carol Lindsley (and by proxy, her girlfriend, Brenda Richardson) to have free rein of the basement, where she orchestrated an adventurous program of exhibitions and actions by the Bay Area vanguard. In just three years, Lindsley presented groundbreaking artists (almost all men), including Bruce Nauman, Terry Fox,*

and Howard Fried, who hold a significant place in the development of Conceptualism.

SK: I brought the finished painting down to Carol and Brenda, and they're used to my Conceptual stuff. They're both looking at it. They're not saying anything.

JS: They're used to your Conceptual work, and here's a trippy sunset painting.

SK: [laughs] Yes. I've always looked for ways to remove irony from my work. My goal is to remove it completely. In fact, if I could achieve that just once, that would be fine; I'd be able to stop thinking about it.

Ironically, I suspect he's exaggerating.

Anyway, this guy walks in while we're looking at the painting, and he's not saying anything. He walks by and looks at me and looks at the painting again. He just stands there between us and the painting for about 15 minutes without moving. When he left, Carol and Brenda said, "What just happened?"

I said, "He was stoned on LSD. The painting was activated for him way more so than normal."

So Carol said, "I think we might want to show this." And Brenda said, "Yeah, I think we might." And so that was it. That's actually exactly how I got that show.

Sunset *was exhibited with a series of what Kaltenbach called "space collages" — multilayered arabesques and "the only artworks I ever did that everybody wanted." No images of those works or the exhibition appear to*

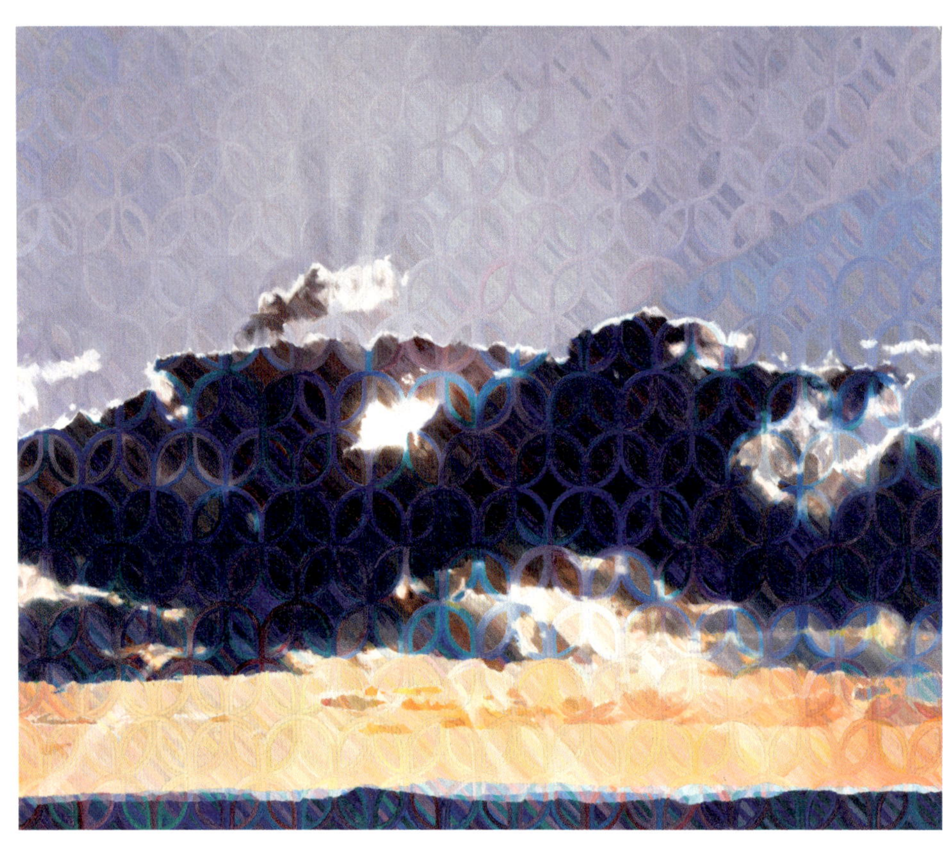

Stephen Kaltenbach, *Sunset*, 1970
Oil on board, 20 × 24 inches (plus detail, opposite)
Collection of the Crocker Art Museum

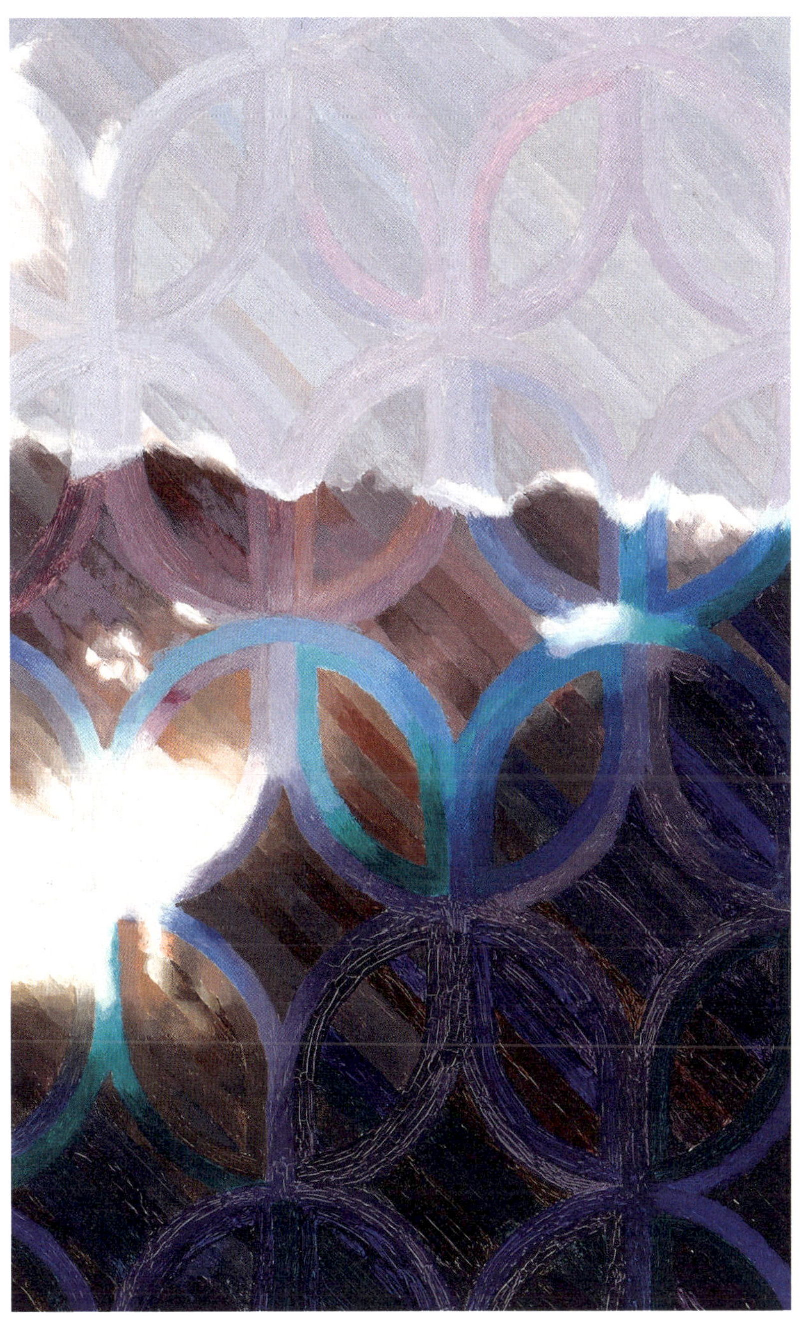

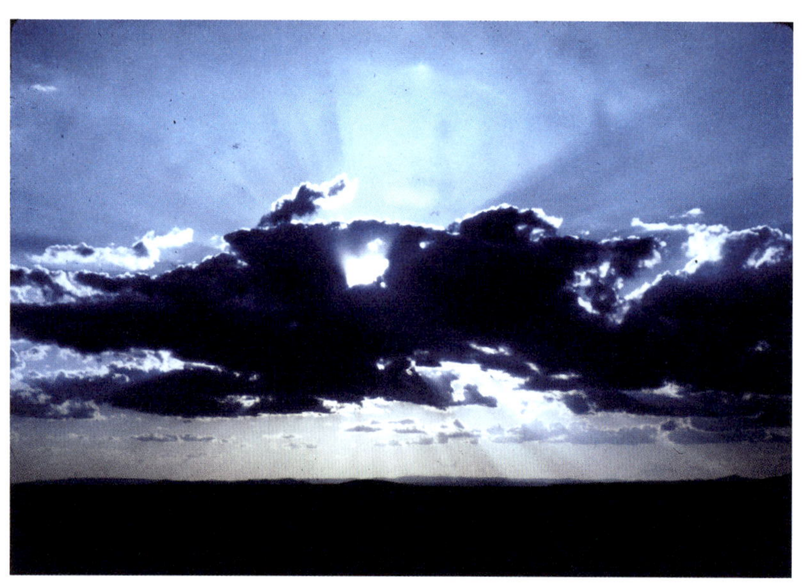

(top) Stephen Kaltenbach, Photographic reference for *Sunset*, 1968,
Courtesy the artist; (bottom) Stephen Kaltenbach, *Sunset* pattern study,
ca.1970, Collection of the artist

*have survived, though the show subsequently traveled
to Palley's gallery in New York.*

SK: I came back and worked another year in New York. But when
the shooting at Kent State happened and the School of Visual Arts
closed down early, I was thinking that if I was going to pursue the
pattern painting, I really needed to leave town.

*The May 4, 1970, murder of four unarmed college
students at Kent State in Ohio triggered a nationwide
strike that forced hundreds of colleges and universities
to close.*

Then finally in 1970, I left New York. I left with the very clear
intention to maintain my career, but make a private turn, do the
work I would have done anyway. I came to Sacramento, where I
lived for a year, worked at Sacramento State, and prepared for the
next painting.

My desire was strong enough to make it OK to leave town and
abandon the career path I was on for one that was really different.
I felt like I needed to be able to go away and hide for a decade.
It was really appealing to me because I was negating my accom-
plishments and the progress I was making in terms of building a
reputation and pursuing a career.

Lee Lozano and I both left as art actions. Lozano was dis-
gusted, or just angry — at least that's how it was expressed. I'm
not really comfortable with making a blanket statement because
she is a pretty tricky woman. I don't know exactly the depth of
her intentions, although I did know her as well, I think, as anybody at the time.

It's difficult to overstate the late 1960s mind meld of Kaltenbach and his friend Lee Lozano, the resolute painter-turned-Conceptualist who embraced life-as-art in a manner that exceeded, inspired, and frightened many of her colleagues, mostly men. In addition to making paintings and works on paper, in 1967 she began to log her observations and declarations in a series of small, wire-bound notebooks, enacting many of them as artworks. She called this LIFE-ART — art to be lived rather than objectified. She sometimes transferred ideas to larger pieces of paper, which were displayed as artworks.

In the spring of 1969, for example, she initiated Grass Piece, *in which she attempted to "STAY HIGH ALL DAY, EVERY DAY. SEE WHAT HAPPENS." Amid self-observations regarding changes in tolerance, she then decides on her next piece: "GO WITHOUT GRASS FOR THE SAME AMOUNT OF TIME."*

And just down the page: "I'LL END THE <u>GRASS PIECE</u> WITH A FANFARE: A CAP OF MESCALINE KALTENBACH GAVE ME. (MAY 2, 69)"

A pair of downtowners high on the possibilities (and impossibilities) of merging life with art, Kaltenbach's and Lozano's ideas are deeply entwined. Who can say which came first, or how, in this case, to measure firsts? She was a decade older, and while they did not "date" per se, her journals reflect a definite and sustained intimacy. In February of 1970, she writes of her "OVERWHELMING LOVE" for Kaltenbach, "WHICH IS NOT FRIEND, NOT SEX, NOT CATEGORY, JUST <u>LOVE</u>."

SK: When I was living in New York in 1967 and '68, I was beginning to see the possibilities, along with a lot of other artists around the world, of the force of ideas and the power they had for aesthetic expression. I observed artists who seemed to be getting a good gallery, getting in a museum show. It was so clear to me how artists were, everything from just being in New York, schmoozing with art professionals, writers, museum and gallery people. Everything seemed directed toward reputation enhancement. There's a certain level, I think, of boredom that begins to set in when you're a very successful artist, and you're making a show and the work is all of a certain character.

I thought, *Well, I'll just go straight to the public.* That was when I began to build the "Protocol of Opposites" as a way to directly show my work.

The "Protocol of Opposites" is no doubt foundational in the artist's telling of his own story and indeed presages his return to California (and the far side of art world anonymity). But its history and specifics are elusive. Rather than an artwork, it's more like an attitude or approach — a stance, a way for him to organize his thoughts and sanction various art-related actions.

That said, it's hard to know when to capitalize certain words across the life of Kaltenbach's mind. Did he understand the "Protocol of Opposites" as such at the time, and if so, is it an artwork? It may be a Protocol, a "protocol," a Protocol, or simply a protocol. Or none of the above. He seems to describe the very same approach as "opposite actions," a somewhat less arresting title than "Protocol of Opposites," in a previously written statement. It may be most accurate to say that it is narratively essential for Kaltenbach in understanding his own trajectory and something of a lifeline, whether or not it was invented in 1967 or some decades later. It is capitalized and rendered with quotation marks throughout this text.

JS: From what I've read, your "Protocol of Opposites" was not just about moving away from institutional validation or formal and stylistic norms; it was also intended to screw with your own growing reputation.

SK: Exactly. It was my intention to screw with my reputation. Having a reputation opens doors, right? That affects a number of things. It's likely to make more money available to you, to make your work more visible, make it appear more professional or prestigious.

"I came to New York for a reputation," Kaltenbach plainly stated in a 1970 Artforum *interview with Cindy Nemser. And build a reputation he did. His very first New York gallery appearance, in fact, was 9 at Leo Castelli, a 1968 exhibition organized by fellow artist Robert Morris at the Castelli Warehouse featuring Eva Hesse, Bruce Nauman, Alan Saret, and Richard Serra, among others. Though the show ran for just two weeks (December 4-28), it has taken on considerable art historical importance with regards to the development of sculpture and installation art.*

In 1969 alone, Kaltenbach's work was featured in 11 group exhibitions, including at notable galleries such as Paula Cooper and Dwan, and in One Month, *a show in the form of a calendar organized by enterprising*

Conceptual art instigator Seth Siegelaub. There was also a Conceptual survey in Leverkusen, Germany, and Live in Your Head: When Attitudes Become Form, *a seminal show of contemporary art organized by pioneering Swiss curator Harald Szeemann in his country's Kunsthalle Berne. Most significantly, Kaltenbach had a solo presentation at the Whitney Museum of American Art. A year later, the artist's work appeared at the Museum of Modern Art in New York in an important show called* Information, *orchestrated by Kynaston McShine.*

SK: When I enacted the "Protocol," I felt freer to do things that either couldn't or shouldn't be done. I felt I was directly interacting with the art establishment's sense of right and wrong.

STONE MAPLE

SK: After *Sunset* I decided to paint a bigger photograph and pattern combination, a 30-by-34 1/2-inch painting from a photograph I found that I liked of a maple tree. I called it *Stone Maple*. I tried to vary the hues a lot, just to kind of see how far away I could go from color reality and still have it work visually as a trcc image.

I actually painted it on a piece of plastic called phenolic plastic, which so far hasn't proven to be disastrous although I noticed the oil paint of certain colors is fracturing, covered with this fine layer of cracks. I'm sure I should have painted on canvas, but oh well.

Lightweight and durable, phenolic plastics are held together with resin largely made from phenol and formaldehyde. They were first manufactured under the trade name Bakelite, and before the mid-1980s, a large percentage contained asbestos.

Stone Maple *is both trippier and more sure-footed than* Sunset; *its verso appropriately titles the work both* Stone *and* Stoned. *Either way, the title is a fiction; while sugar, silver, and Japanese maples exist, there is no stone variety.*

The painting depicts a tree split into two trunks; a smaller branch extends between them, and golden light illuminates foreground leaves and background sky. The perspective is upward-facing and fully encompassed. It evokes the experience of looking through a dense forest on a sunny day, and the perceptual extremes of light and dark as branches extend in every direction.

Look closer and there's a total network of concentric, heart-shaped rings glowing blue, red, green, yellow, purple — colors in countless shades of themselves, their tones, values, and hues changing in a dizzying array. The surface is waxy and transparent. Once runny, it's now frozen, cracked, and mosaiclike.

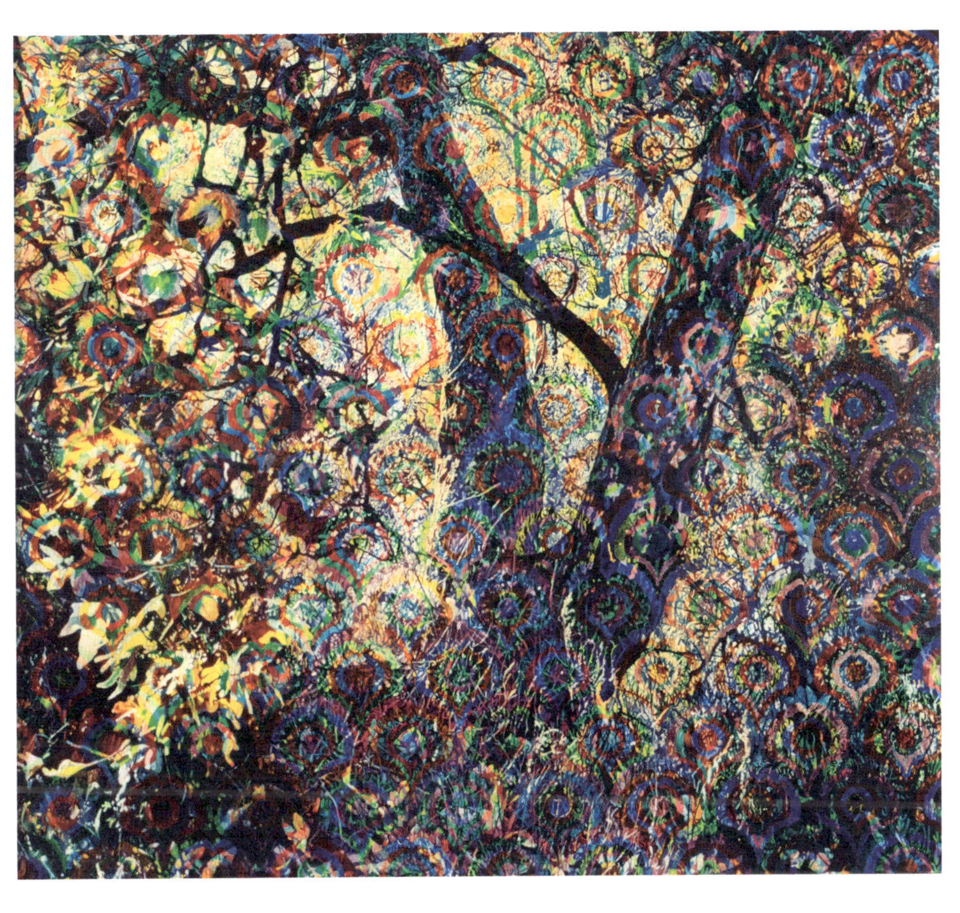

Stephen Kaltenbach, *Stone Maple*, 1971-1972
Oil on plastic, 30 × 34 1/2 inches, Collection of the artist

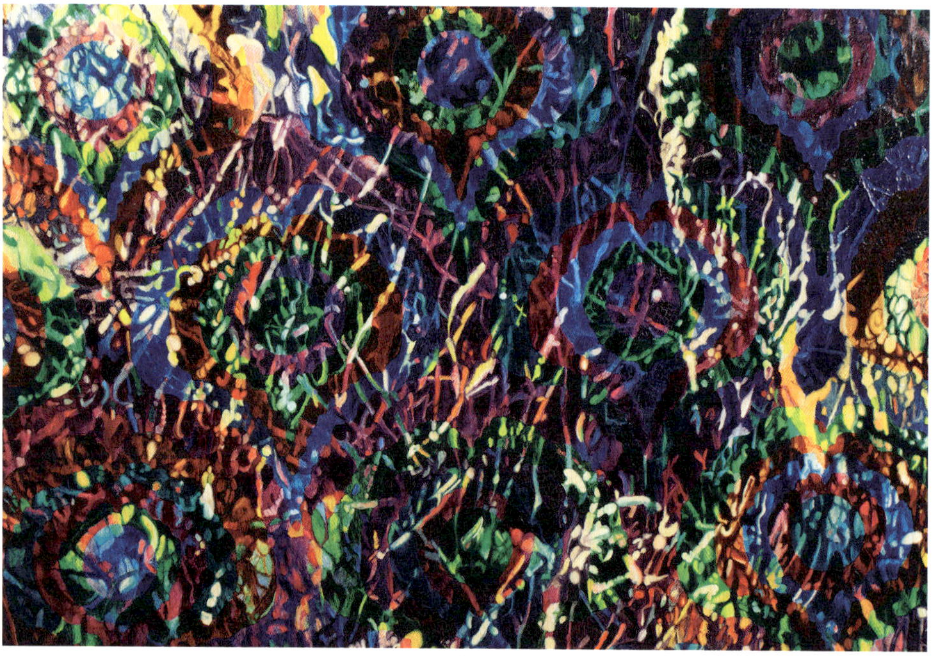

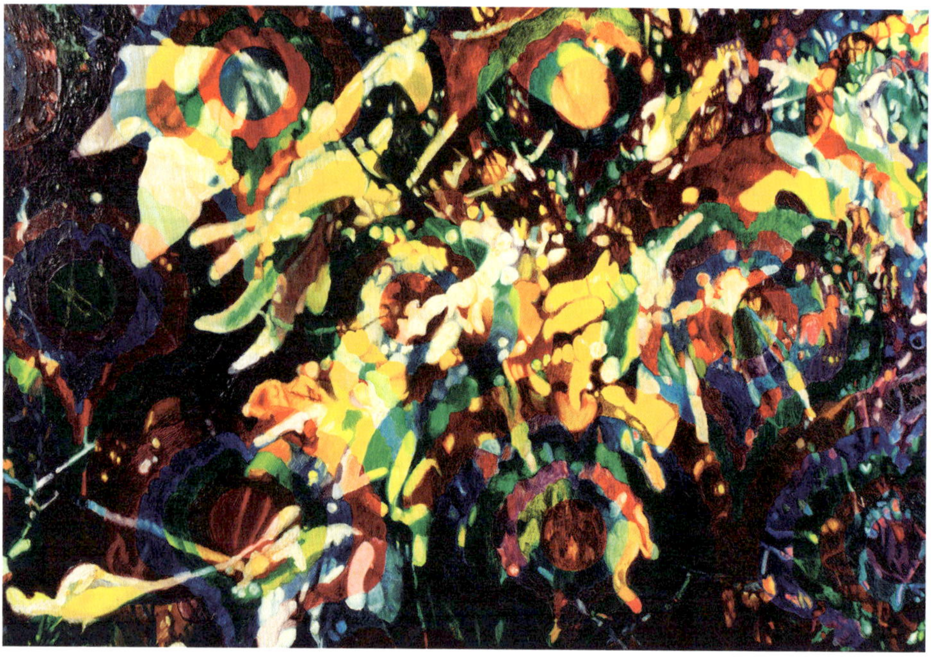

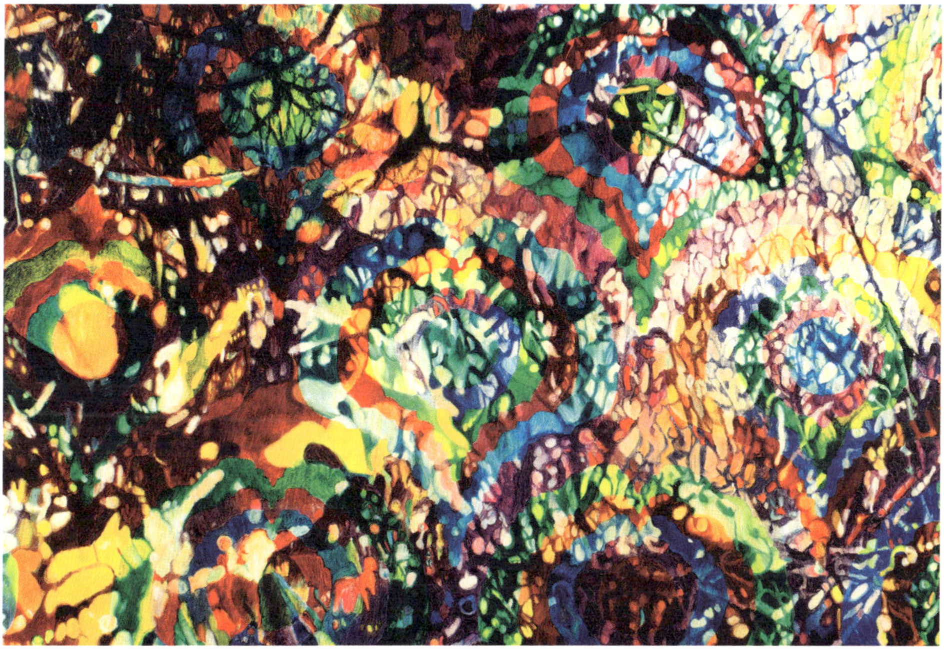

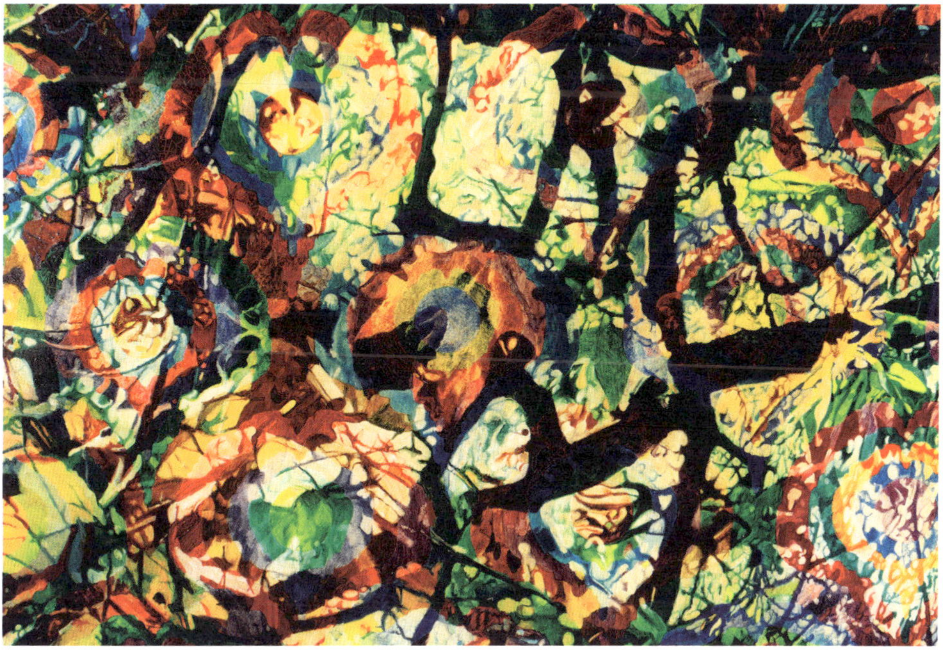

Stone Maple (details)

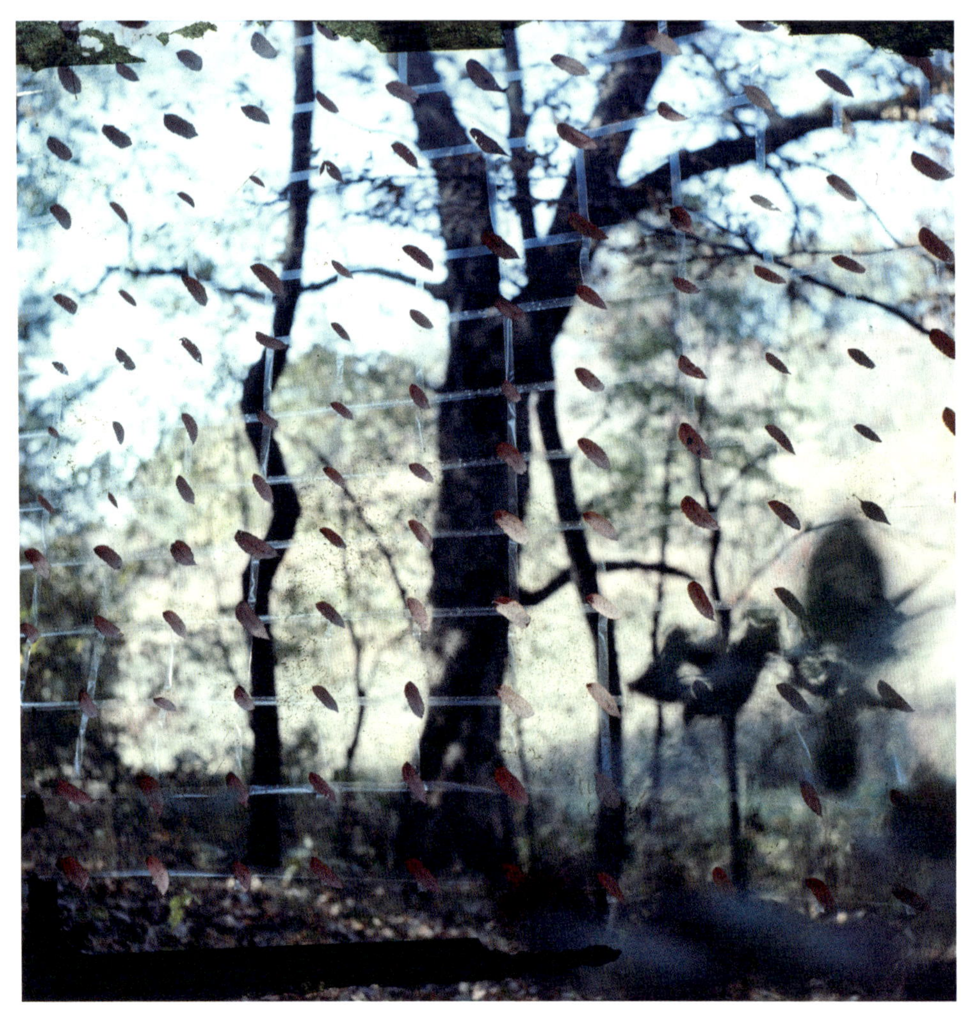

Stephen Kaltenbach, *Stone Maple* pattern study, ca.1971
Collection of the artist

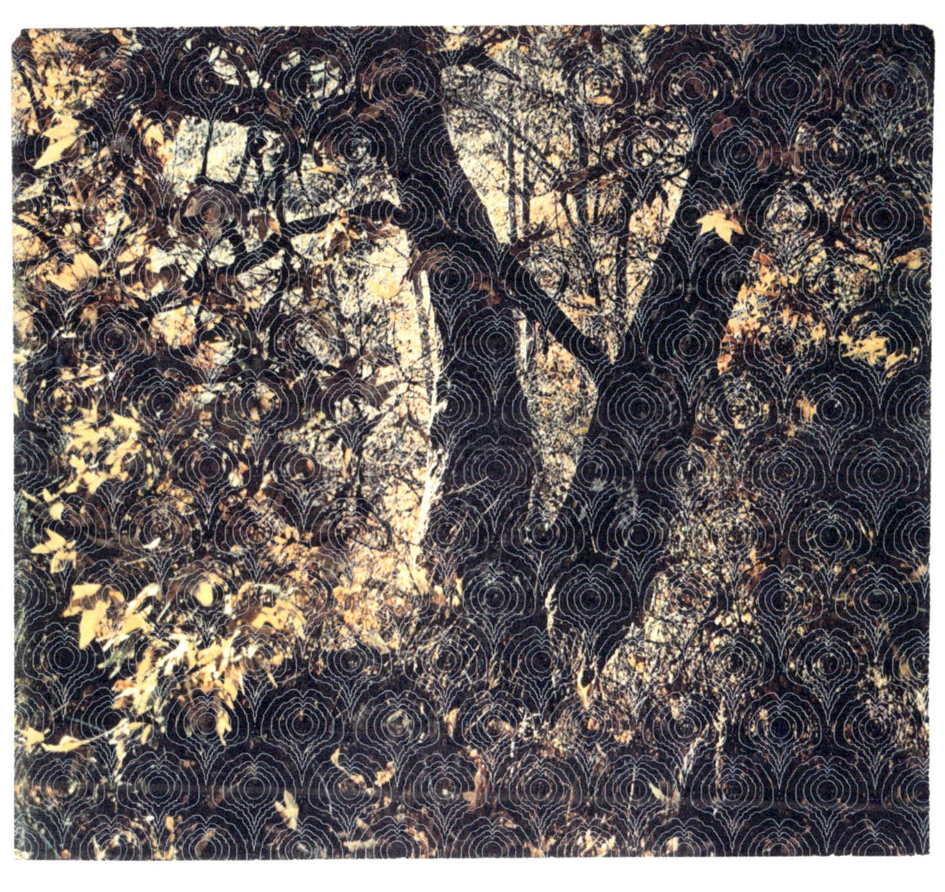

Stephen Kaltenbach, *Stone Maple* in progress, ca.1971
Collection of the artist

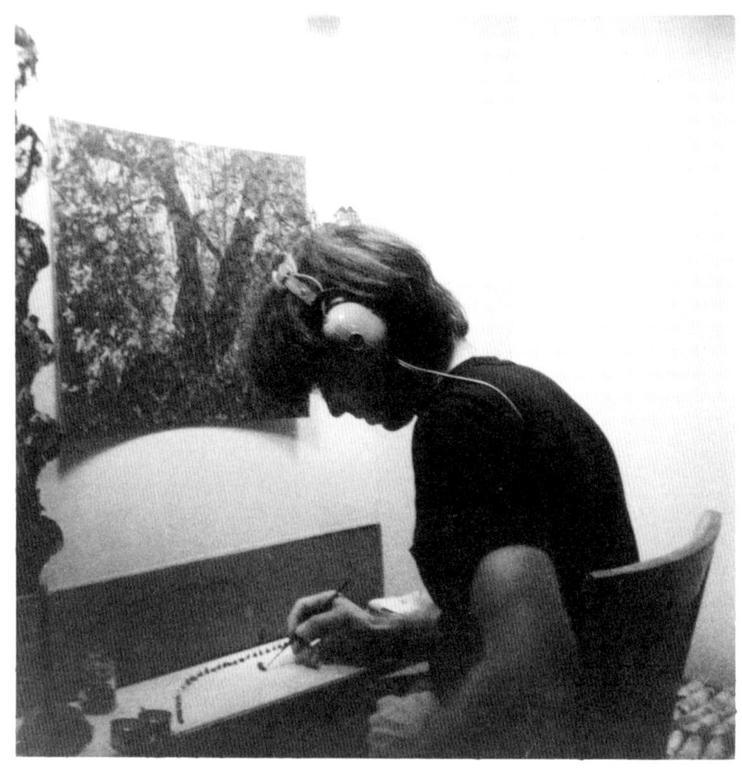

Stone Maple in progress, Madison, Wisconsin, 1971
(printed September 1972), Photo: Nancy Mark, Courtesy the artist

SK: In California, I was doing sculpture and Conceptual art, continuing to do what I had been doing in New York, but just doing it privately.

Like many of Kaltenbach's thoughts and actions, this one directly echoes a Lozano work called Painting Piece: *"NOW I REALIZE THAT THE WAVE SERIES MUST BE KEPT PRIVATE, WITHIN THE STUDIO, TO BE AVAILABLE ONLY TO THOSE PEOPLE I LIKE ENOUGH TO INVITE OVER, OR THOSE WHO HAVE THE CHUTZPAH TO COME UNINVITED. (APRIL 3, 1969) MAKE ANOTHER KIND OF ART FOR THE OUTSIDE WORLD."*

Kaltenbach's Conceptualism broke the surface at least once. A March 1975 Artforum *review of a three-person exhibition at Berkeley's University Art Museum (alongside Stephen David and Howard Fried) that included* Stone Maple *mentioned a letter from a lawyer on view, outlining how Kaltenbach might designate his work "owner-less" by perpetually loaning it to museums. And when the same work was exhibited alongside* Portrait of My Father *four years later at the Crocker, art-curious readers of the February 16, 1979,* Davis Enterprise-Weekend *edition may have learned that the work — here referred to as* Maple Trees *— was indeed declared "legally ownerless" in 1973. An ownerless painting, financially speaking, would be rendered worthless and impossible to insure.*

SK: After a year in California, I moved to Madison, Wisconsin, as a teacher and artist in residence for two semesters. While I was there, I was in the library and saw a William Morris book about patterns that hadn't been checked out since the late 1940s. One of the things I read was that "there are no new patterns."

When I came back to Davis, I got an Angora Persian cat named Teddy. I decided I wanted to paint something with hair, and I wanted to paint it big enough so I could paint individual hairs. At the time I thought Teddy was the perfect subject.

Then my sister sent me a snapshot of Dad. My mom had let his beard grow, and I had never seen him with a beard. He was unable to walk by himself by that time; he'd had numerous strokes and was bedridden.

Then somehow the decision to paint the cat — to paint the cat or not to paint the cat. *Hey, this guy is painting his cat.* Anyway, I decided to do the portrait of Dad. So I built a stretcher and kept it in my place in Sacramento.

I recognized that painting a portrait — let alone a portrait of the artist's father — was really swimming upstream for a contemporary artist.

It's hard to overstate just how heretical a hallucinogenic painting of Kaltenbach's Persian cat would have read to his recent peers. For a time, this made Teddy an ideal subject, and moving such a specimen from calendar to canvas an irresistible pull for the young contrarian. While distinct modes, Minimalism and Conceptualism were to a great extent defined by their visual and aesthetic austerity, lack of traditional expression, and encouragement of intellectual engagement. It's fair to say that both movements turned their collective back on the grand gestural subjectivity of large-scale painting, and much else.

Kaltenbach was initially quite at home within the rise of idea-based art practices in New York, but his return to California was largely a return to the retinal, both real and chemically conferred. Further, painting his dad was even less of an idea than painting his cat — after all, the formidable representation of a dead or dying man is perhaps the most common subject in the history of painting. In other words, it took imagination to have such little imagination in Kaltenbach's new context.

In order to more fully grapple with his choices and changes, to begin to comprehend those six years in a rural California barn, it's essential to consider his thinking and output in New York — including his thinking as output — and all that he walked away from. He and I discussed five such projects: one impossible to trace (Causal Art Actions); one hypothetical (Street Plaques); one unquestionably material but calling for its own destruction (Time Capsules); one anonymous (Artforum advertisements); and one that trolled "bad" painting (Lord & Taylor Paintings).

SK: When I got to New York at the end of August in 1967, I made a few studio visits with the intention of trying to move another artist's work along just by talking — I thought of this as a "causal art action."

I'd encourage the reader to think of this sentence as perfectly in line with other artworks of the time defined by poetical economy of thought, suggestion of off-screen activity, and disavowal of hard evidence. Consider Lawrence Weiner, who, for example, contributed the following text to Seth Siegalaub's 1969 calendar exhibition: "An object tossed from one country to another." Or Robert Barry, who in the same show submitted the following: "Inert gas series, 1969; Helium (2 cubic feet) Description: Sometime during the morning of March 5, 1969, 2 cubic feet of Helium will be released into the atmosphere." There was air in the air.

JS: How did that project get started?

SK: I showed my slides to Barbara Rose, who happened to be Robert Morris' girlfriend. I remember she went through a whole series of work that I had done as a student and said, "Oh, look at this. Are you in touch with Bob?" I wasn't, but we realized later that we had been doing things in concert.

Barbara Rose (1936–2020) was an American art historian, art critic, curator, and professor. Her criticism focused on 20th century American art, particularly Minimalism, and her hugely influential 1965 essay "ABC Art" defined the historical basis of the movement as explicitly contrary to the aims of Abstract Expressionism: "One might as easily construe the new, reserved impersonality and self-effacing anonymity as a reaction against the self-indulgence of an unbridled subjectivity, just as one might see it in terms of a formal reaction to the excesses of painterliness." This helps explain Kaltenbach's attraction to, and subsequent turn from, neighborhoods like SoHo.

William Smith: How did this essay come about?
Barbara Rose: None of my friends could sell anything, so it was really propaganda for their work.

Robert Morris (1931–2018) was an American artist who worked in dance, sculpture, drawing, painting, film, photography, collage, writing, and more. Regarded as a prominent theorist of Minimalism along with Donald Judd, he also made important contributions to the development of performance, process, land, and installation art. As early as 1961, Morris was developing new, koan-like possibilities for art with the seminal Box with the Sound of Its Own Making, *a small wooden cube that broadcast the sound of its construction — saw, hammer, and all — from inside.*

JS: Did you eventually meet Morris?

SK: Yes, and I attempted a causal art action with him. I thought, OK, *this is a guy who I'll really be able to communicate with,* and so I showed him some work. The first guy I told about my plan was a friend I'd known since I was 16. He said, "You better watch out. People are going to hate you for this if word gets out." And word got out. That was a bad thing.

I had a number of realizations. One was that there was no way to determine the effect your words and observations had on another artist's mind because there is no way to tell where they are in their discovery process. The other was that it's a really bad idea to say anything specific about who you were working with and what you

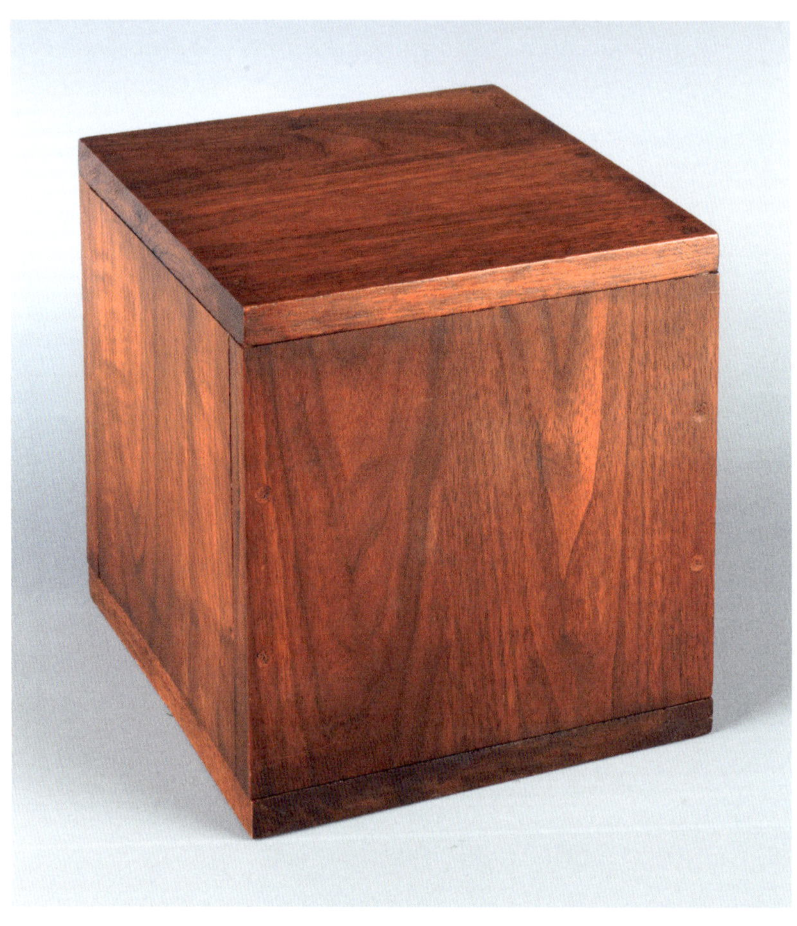

Robert Morris, *Box with the Sound of Its Own Making*, 1961, Wood, internal speaker, Cube: 9 3/4 × 9 3/4 × 9 3/4 inches, With pedestal: 46 × 9 3/4 × 9 3/4 inches, TRT 3.5 hours, Seattle Art Museum, Gift of the Virginia and Bagley Wright Collection, © The Estate of Robert Morris / Artists Rights Society (ARS), New York, Photo: Elizabeth Mann

think you achieved. The experience taught me not to talk about things. It was also a very selfish thing to do.

> *Kaltenbach's exploration of influence reinforced the truth that artists have always taken from each other — both plainly and surreptitiously. What made his approach distinct was its peculiar blend of open-ended dialogue, quasi-scientific observation, and outright manipulation. Notably, his experience didn't teach him not to do it, but instead not to discuss it. In the center of the art world, it seems his goal was to achieve visibility and invisibility in the same breath. Or as he explained to Artforum in 1970: "One of the first things I did when I got to New York was to try to influence Bob's work. It was my first pure causal art work. Most of the first causal work was secret. I documented it, but my ego was so involved I really didn't know how to consider it. I wanted to specify it as an art activity and bring it into the realm of something which could be credited to me."*

JS: Did you do anything differently in those visits than you would have done in any other visits aside from calling it a causal art action?

SK: At the time I was thinking of alchemy. I tried to pass through other people's ideas and vice versa. The artist has the advantage of knowing what they're doing when they're making a work, and a visitor to the studio has the advantage of a free perspective, not locked into a specific approach.

For instance, you go to another artist and you have an idea of how you want his work to change, and you say something to try to cause that to happen. That's the dark view of what I was doing.

Another view, and the one that I held, was that this is something that existed anyway, that artists who were friends would visit each other and kick around ideas in the studio that were based on the hopes of moving each other's work forward.

Lozano was up to very similar thinking in at least two journal entries:

"PARTY PIECE (OR PARANOIA PIECE)
DESCRIBE YOUR CURRENT WORK TO A FAMOUS BUT FAILING ARTIST FROM THE EARLY 60'S. WAIT TO SEE WHETHER HE BOOSTS* ANY OF YOUR IDEAS.
(MARCH 15, 1969)
* HOIST, COP, STEAL"

"PASS ON ALL YOUR IDEAS PIECE – (STARTED MAY 17, 69) [ALSO CALLED THE ROBT MORRIS PIECE]"

SK: In New York I saw brass and bronze plaques laid in the sidewalk that said things like "Utilities," "Permission Revocable," whatever. They're just like urban nature. I began to think of making plaques that would have much more surrealistic or mysterious meanings.

The idea of Minimalism was a reduction or simplification of form. My idea was to hide the nature of the work in the sidewalk someplace. If it was the word "fire" or "water," then it could be taken as municipal, just the kind of stuff the city will put out there, where the utilities are. If it's a word like "blood" or "flesh," then it becomes surrealistic and gains a certain amount of poetic mystery.

I began to think about my life and about how on Greene Street, where I lived, there were all kinds of people and industry all over the place. If somebody came across the words "earth" or "skin," it probably would stop them; I'd have them in a state that's different from the state that they're in when they're in Paris and going to the Pompidou or something, whatever. Right?

JS: Yes, they're unprepared for an official art experience in that context.

SK: If they're prepared to look at art, that's what they're going to see. I think I had them at a disadvantage, or in a slightly more vulnerable state that was ultimately to both of our advantages.

JS: I wonder about your relationship to anonymity, especially because hypothetical viewers wouldn't be able to determine authorship even if they wanted to.

SK: Certainly, anonymity was part of Minimalism; reducing or removing authorship seemed to have a very strong effect on the work in certain circumstances. I was not yet aware of how good the establishment was at pointing out who the anonymous person was.

JS: But was it important to you at the time that neighbors or neighborhood artists would find out 10 days later that it was you?

SK: I would like to say that I'd much rather stay anonymous; however …

JS: You're in New York for a reason.

SK: [laughs] Yes. Those are unresolved questions. I considered them and I had enough awareness to realize what I was thinking and how I was feeling, and yet it seemed as though there should be some things that remain anonymous.

The pieces I made required collectors to complete them by placing them in public sidewalks. If there was no limit to their appearance in the city, then there was no way to know the piece's edges. It's creating a work of art for which there is no known definition. You can't circumscribe its edges.

In theory, Kaltenbach's anonymous bronze plaques democratized encounters with art by withholding traditional context generally afforded an art-going audience. That said, while many street plaque images were reprinted in a 1970 Artforum *interview, exactly none were placed in the ground. That gives a sense of where the artist's allegiances lay at the time, and the distance — or the collapse of distance — between the material and immaterial in his imagination.*

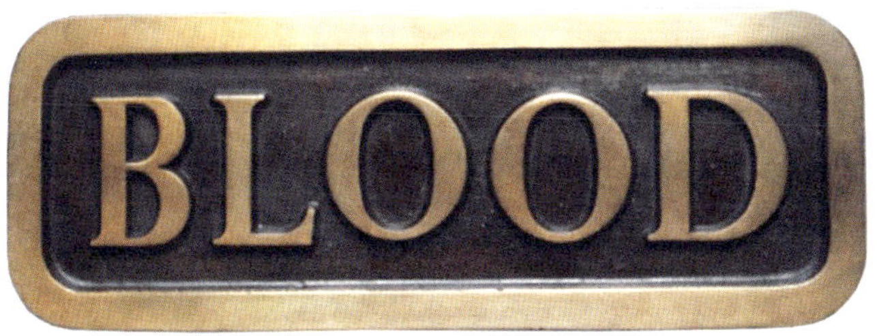

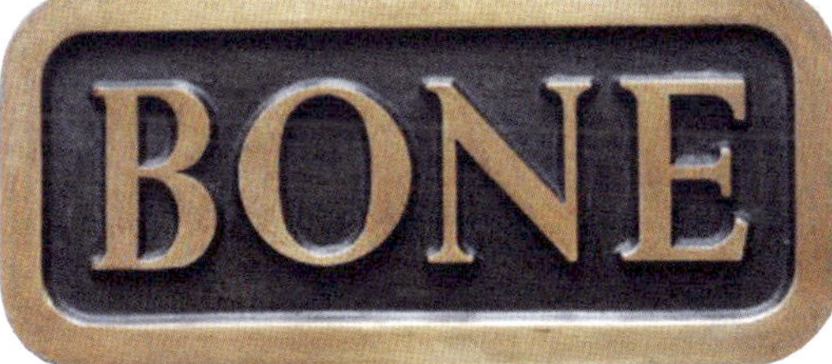

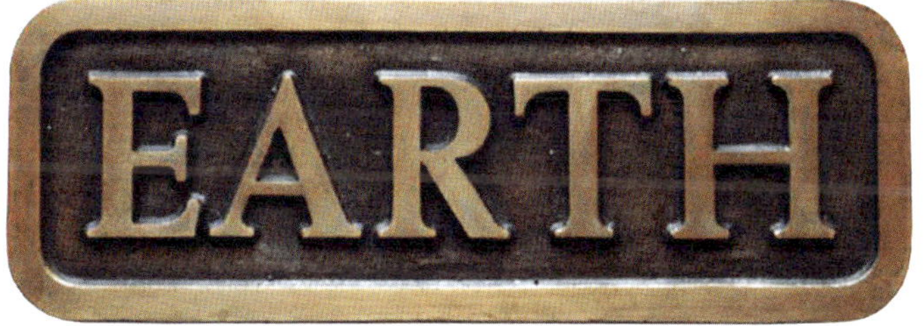

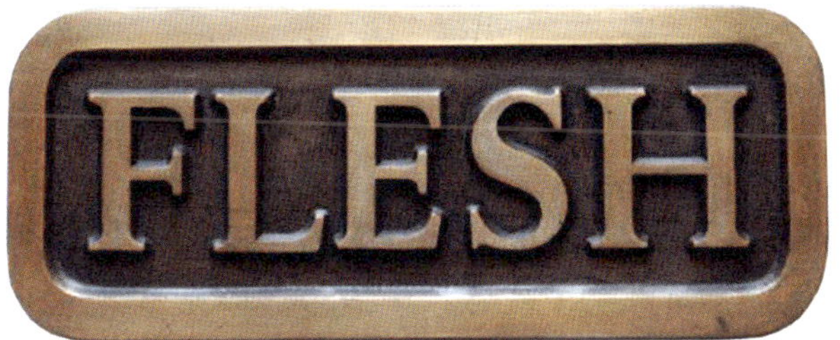

Stephen Kaltenbach, *Sidewalk Plaques*, 1968-69/2010/2019
Dimensions variable, Collection of the artist

TIME CAPSULES

His Time Capsules *are metal objects, mainly cylinders, bearing ostensibly straightforward instructions on their exterior that often carry a mandate to expire.*

BRUCE NAUMAN RETAIN POSSESSION
OF THIS CAPSULE DO NOT OPEN UNTIL
NOTIFIED

BURY WITH THE ARTIST

MUSEUM OF MODERN ART TO BE OPENED
AT THE REQUEST OR DEATH OF STEPHEN
KALTENBACH

OPEN AFTER JAN. 1 2025 A.D.

OPEN AFTER JAN. 1 2075 A.D.

OPEN AFTER MY DEATH

SK: What I found very interesting with the *Time Capsules* was the idea of making these objects knowing that they were going to either private or public collections, and that if their instructions were followed through, they would actually destroy the container.

If you want to make stuff and not necessarily have it be seen, what do you do? If you hide something, then how do you show it? I came to terms with the fact that you're showing a hidden thing. The work was hiding the nature of the work.

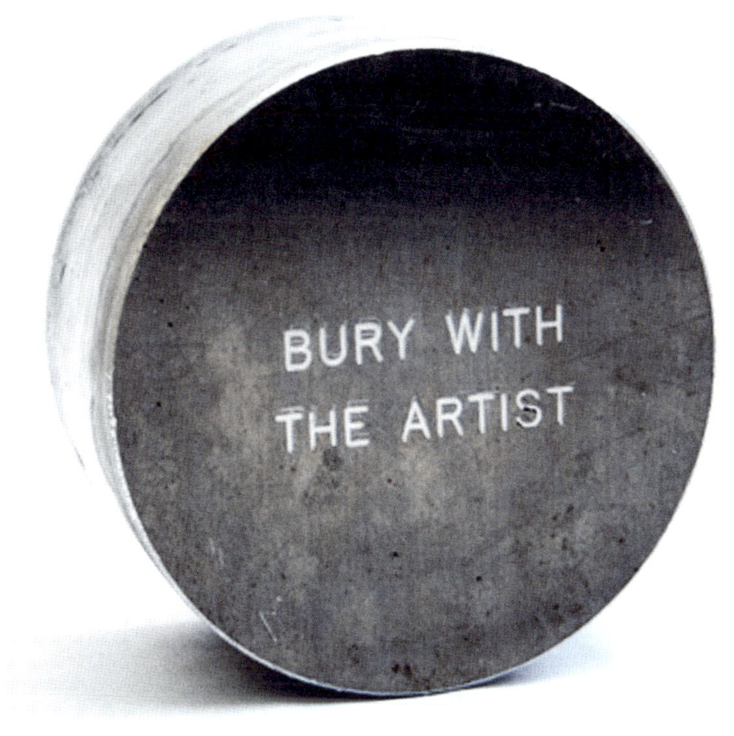

Stephen Kaltenbach, *BURY WITH THE ARTIST*, 1968
Aluminum and unknown contents, 5 × 5 × 2 3/4 inches.

Kaltenbach's commercial art dealer, the gallery Another Year in LA, has published many of his writings on its website, including a statement that begins, "The idea for these works was generated without apparent conceptual lineage while I was a grad student."

Christo and Jean-Claude, Marcel Duchamp, and Man Ray are just four 20th century artists who played with similar ideas before 1970. Before and beyond that, and in countless iterations from the pyramids to the avant-garde, perhaps a secret lies at the heart of all artwork.

The text goes on to describe the work's intended audience, an increasingly important subject to him:

"For the Time Capsules, *there were several target audiences. First was the curator or collector. They were and still are faced with the choice of having minimal information about the work or of having to go against everything their training and good sense has always dictated: preserve the work; basically, never saw it in two. The second target group was the writer/historian. They were encouraged to do what they like to do best: mount investigations into the probable dynamics and content of these pieces. But for them, in a sense, history would be running backwards. Instead of the artist's motives and intentions fading through time into the past, this information was waiting to be discovered in the future by simply following the artist's instructions. Certainly art viewers would be at the receiving end of this secretive work as well. My thought was that they would be given free rein to use their imagination to complete the work; a minimal piece indeed. I and my [sic] reputation*

were the last perceived targets of the work because of the possible actions, or lack thereof, elicited by these pieces. I was interested to see whether a work, which maintained secrecy over time, would hold its interest until it was opened or if it was never opened. […] These time delay works were all in agreement with a protocol I was operating under which I referred to as 'opposite actions'. Obviously, one of my primary interests was to initiate original movement in the flow of art world ideation. One of the most likely ways to cause this, I decided, was to isolate natural actions, and then try to find a way of doing, making, or being that was most unlike that; for example, hiding instead of showing. The Time Capsules *fit that very well."*

SK: I gave Barbara Rose a time capsule to be opened when, as written on the capsule, I "achieve national prominence" as an artist; it turned out to be a good strategy because she lost it. I spent three months preparing the contents for it; it was my first capsule, and I was ambitious about what I wanted to do with it. I spent time doing something really hard.

The artist appears to have remade, retitled, and redated the piece some years later. And at some point he redated all Time Capsules *"1970–present."*

The Time Capsules *transform speculation itself into an artistic medium and tend to highlight the ways in which museums traffic in posterity, largely defining who and what becomes art historical, and when.*

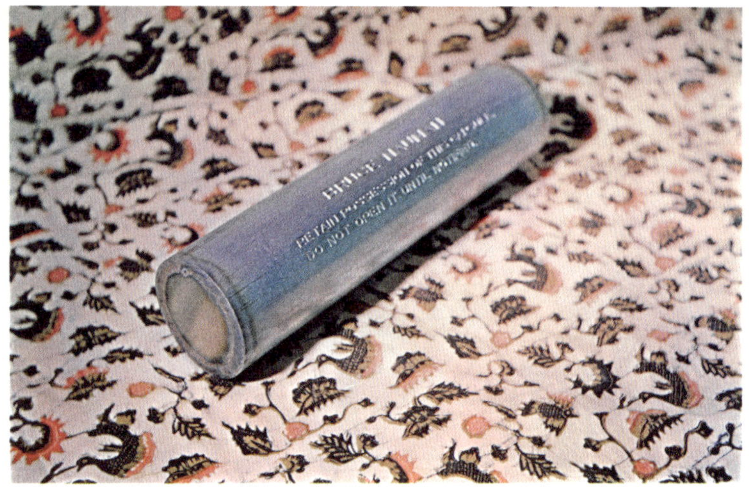

many of the projects I set up and get going turn out to be very small scale, and, at least from one point of view, are miserable failures.

A good example of this is the tread design I made for the astronauts. As you know, last year there was a great deal of talk about the astronauts' an involvement in a secondary aspect than I wanted to have. So now if I have an idea for a new kind of sanding disc or a new toy or a new means of advertising, I write it down, as tersely as possible, and ship it out to someone who might be interested in it. But I don't see the results, and thing else—working without a return or with a purely imagined reaction. I think that a lot of feedback is unnecessary or can lead you to things that aren't interesting or confusing. You don't have to deal with these things when you don't have feedback. You don't have to deal with reality

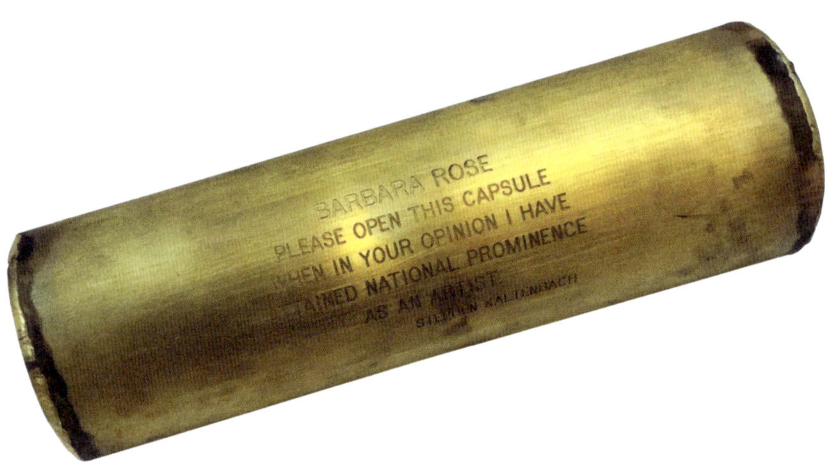

(top) *Artforum*, November 1970, Pictured within: Stephen Kaltenbach, *Time Capsule for Bruce Nauman*, 1968, Steel and unknown contents, From *An Interview with Stephen Kaltenbach*, Courtesy *Artforum*; (bottom) Stephen Kaltenbach, *Time Capsule for Barbara Rose*, 1967—68/2016, Brass and unknown contents, 3 × 3 × 10 1/2 inches, Collection of the artist

From November 1968 to the end of 1969, Kaltenbach placed a series of 12 enigmatic advertisements in Artforum *magazine, where typical ads announced exhibitions, promoted artists, or simply printed the name of the purchasing gallery. His anonymous insertions mainly included directives — "Perpetrate a hoax," "Smoke" — and also more obtuse statements — "You are me," "Johnny Appleseed" — functioning as what he called "mini-manifestos" that turned the magazine's commercial space into raw Conceptual terrain. His ads functioned simultaneously as artwork, critique, and a kind of performance that unfolded through both space and time, highlighting how art world status was constructed through tiny blocks of two-dimensional real estate.*

SK: When I put the ads in *Artforum*, it was anonymous; that lasted less than a week. Many people were calling up the magazine asking who put the artworks in. The man who handled advertising finally got a hold of me and said, "Look, there are requests about this. Can we tell them or not?" It was never an issue for me. I said, "Well, sure." I knew that they would be found out, but I was happy that they operated initially on an anonymous basis. There was no announcement that I had done it; it was just done. I also enjoyed that it became difficult or impossible to determine its effects. And there was still the moment of encounter.

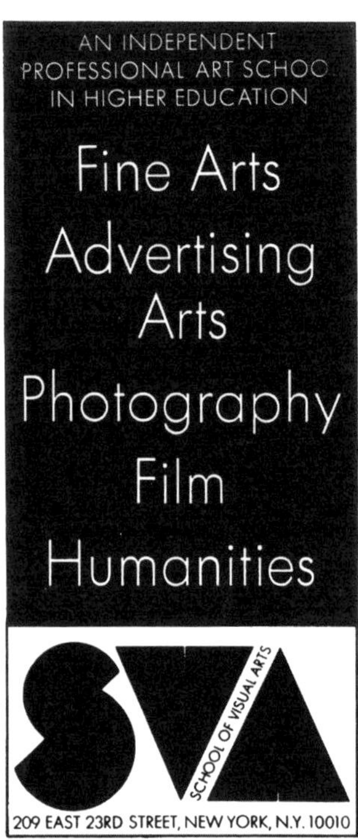

AN INDEPENDENT
PROFESSIONAL ART SCHOOL
IN HIGHER EDUCATION
Fine Arts
Advertising Arts
Photography
Film
Humanities
SVA
SCHOOL OF VISUAL ARTS
209 EAST 23RD STREET, NEW YORK, N.Y. 10010

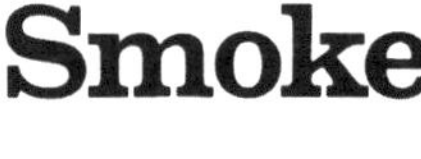

Smoke

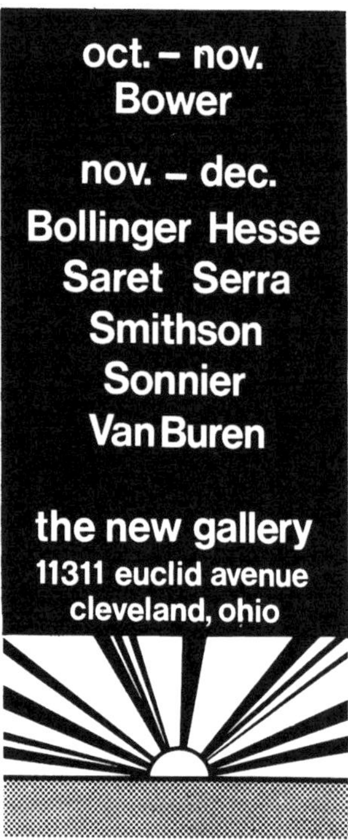

oct. – nov.
Bower
nov. – dec.
Bollinger Hesse
Saret Serra
Smithson
Sonnier
Van Buren
the new gallery
11311 euclid avenue
cleveland, ohio

Trip.

his is perhaps the crux of
for this is not Pop art, but
y sophisticated, self-con-
ltivated pseudo-Primitiv-
ed by a very gifted ama-
ed of broad art-historical
cal awarenesses and acute,
brilliant, technical com-
, who has· much to say
Primitivism and Pop art,
as, as well, a genuine in-
with his pictorial subject
r. Fiscus, who began
1967, is an admitted self-
ce and avocational ama-
with the difference that
essionally a Humanities
has been for some years
lty of a major art school
rancisco Art Institute.)
a native Californian with
gs for the grandeur and
estern landscape and Pa-
seascape, both of which
with intimate familiarity
r of series, each devoted
n traversed by some well-
ic highway, the road map
of which captions the se-
while Fiscus may whim-
ge in an occasional syn-
erbole, as an aside in the
ry tongue-in-cheek vein
comments-on-art, his total
ar from merely the extrav-
n it might appear to be at
nce. For he clearly regards
e challenge of making the
que to his pseudo-Primi-
natization communicate
responses to these pan-
us, his considerable self-
insights and resources

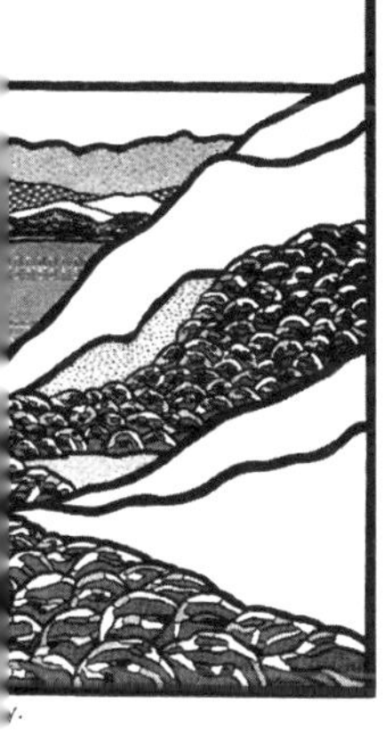

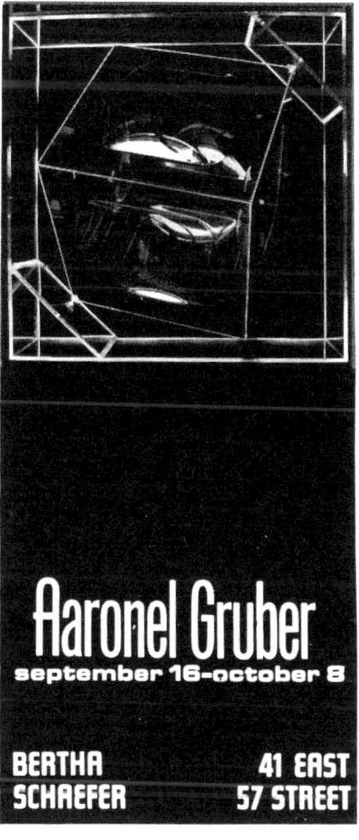

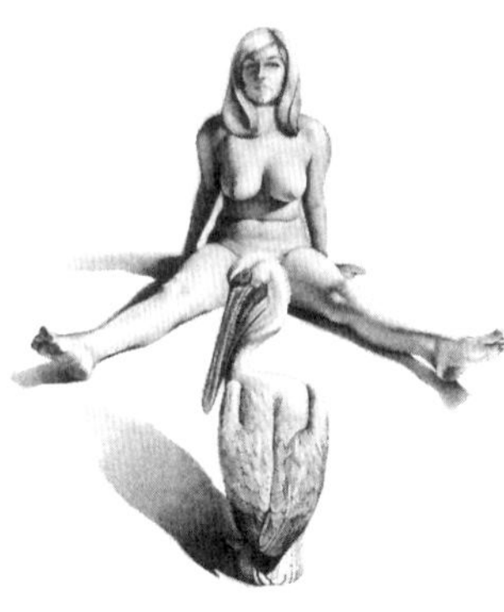

Mel Ramos, *Leta and the White Pelican*, o/c, 60x52'', 1969. David Stuart Galleries.

ings, cutely conceals the pubic regions), and bits of print shop embellishment—metallic surfaces, embossing, etc. I found the lithographs unsatisfactory, looking on first glance like record album covers and on second glance like superbly designed institutional advertisements (e.g., Union Carbide making a point about air pollution). But the lithographs suffer not from concept, but merely from being commercial on a pedestrian level; Ramos, however, believes in the paintings, and it is with them we must decide why, in spite of all those compartments of desirability, they seem so soul-less, even ingested tongue-in-cheek. I think it is because, indicating the borders on either side, they are not as bravely crummy as Warhol's silk-screen paintings and not as really whimsical as Ed Ruscha's gunpowder drawings.

TOM HOLLAND's eight new paintings (plus one in the office) called the "Malibu Series" are made from sheets of translucent plastic, liberally and loosely painted with predominantly white, black, or an overall mix like a chalky rainbow. The sizes float in the seven-foot-square neighborhood. The pictures present themselves as extended paintings, a two-dimensional, rectangle-based art (Holland is a painter) rather than a flattened, polychromatic sculpture. The complexity of surface is usually two or three units (units = a felt plane, not each separate physical piece), though the basket-weave paintings seem, on the whole, simpler (one surface) and the moebius-band-addition pictures start jumping off the wall. These paintings are better than Holland's earlier work but, if there is an intended connection in "funk" between the airplanes and telescopes and waterfalls of yesterday, and the loosely carpentered, riveted, bolted and punctured sheets of plastic, it fails—all to the better. The incantations of Cubist formalism are too strong, the drip is too elegant, and the color compromise too knowledgeable (too little chroma and we'd have patinated sculpture, too much and it would destroy the multi-surface readings) for Holland to pretend to any kind of primitivism. He's best in the basket-weave pictures when he stays closest to painting, and forces the reading on those terms, although the moebius-band pictures do usefully contain an old-fashioned figure-ground ambiguity. Perhaps one last thing ought to be noted: there is a slight feeling of stylish eclecticism, *i.e.*, a programmed emulsion of the "right" non-art materials and a timely revival of Abstract Expressionism. There are vague reports aplenty in Los Angeles of other name artists "using" Abstract Expressionism in new work in progress, similar to Lichtenstein's *faux naif* employment of Thirties Moderne.

—PETER PLAGENS

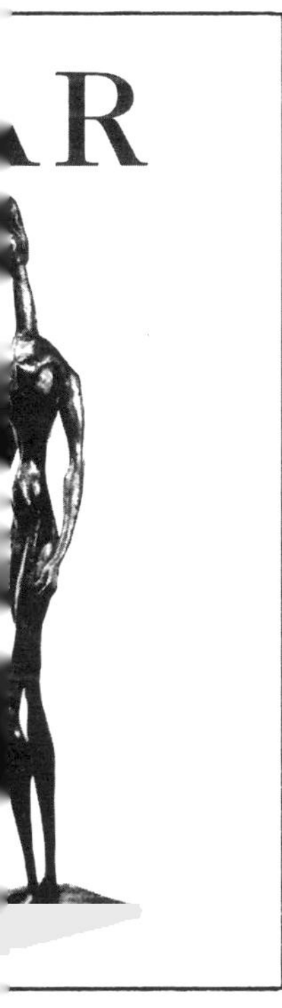

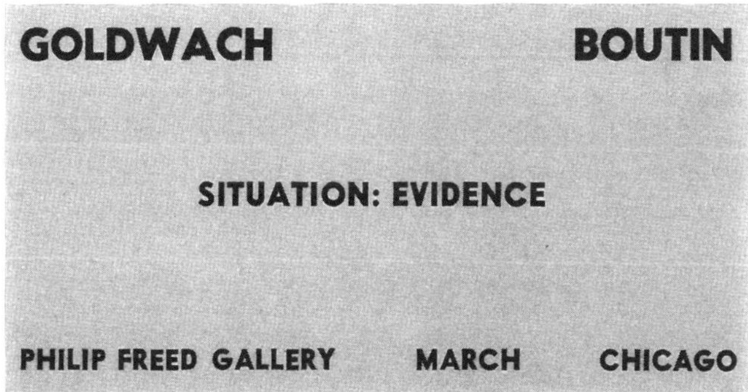

GOLDWACH   BOUTIN

SITUATION: EVIDENCE

PHILIP FREED GALLERY   MARCH   CHICAGO

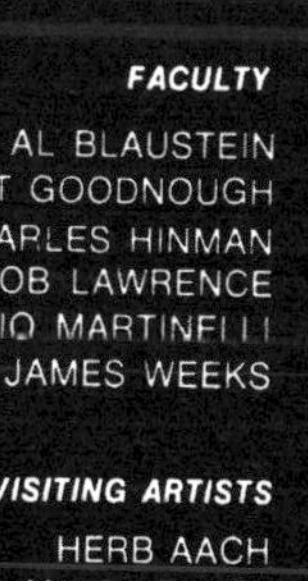

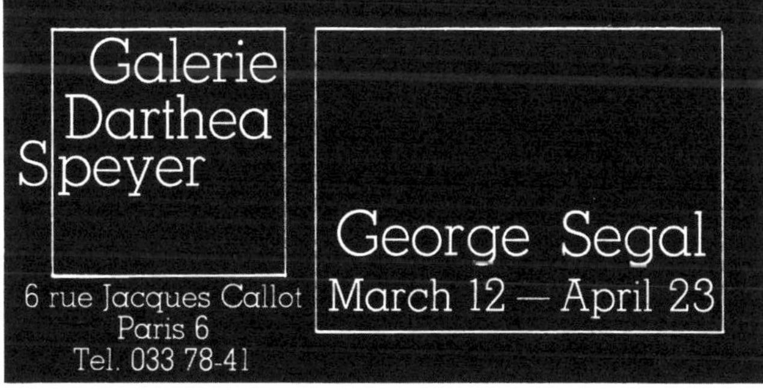

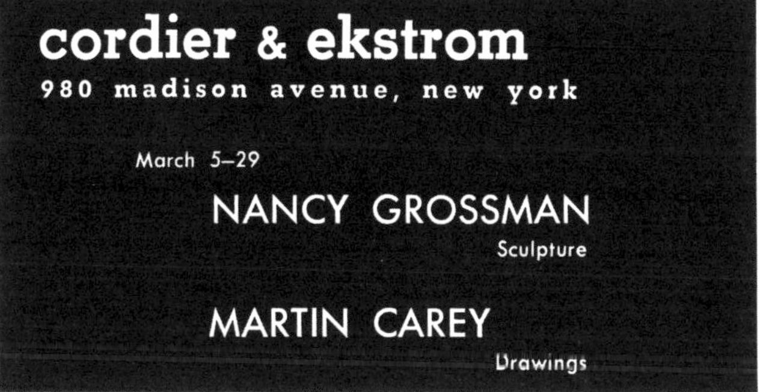

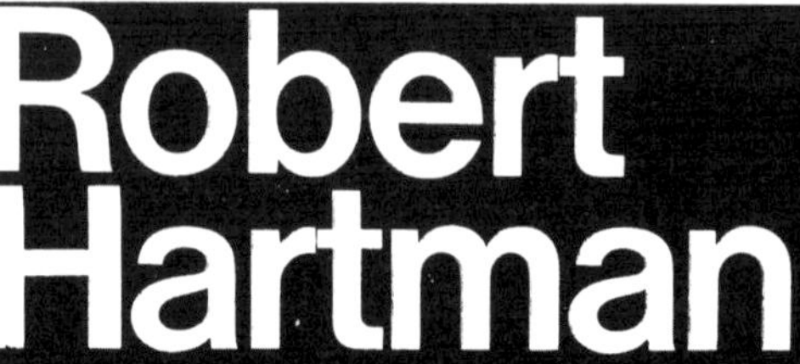

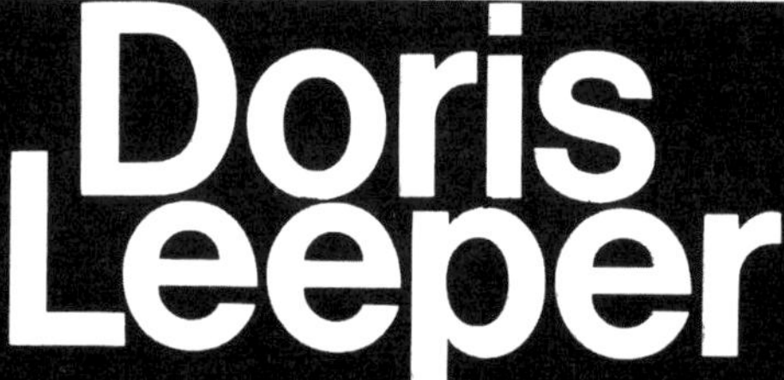

Perpetrate **a hoax**

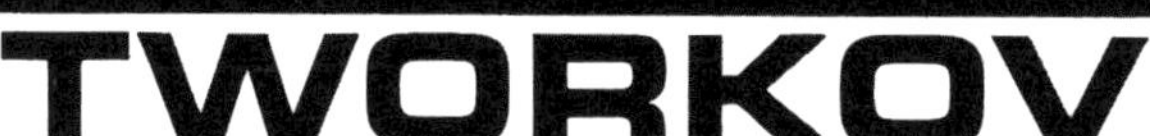

makes them. They're summing
names, they tie a knot around
whole personality, and suggest
kind of bravura signature that
derlines itself. Jeff Carter, Tess Mil
Mathew Garr, Guino Rinaldo, B
Kennelley, Johnny Lovo, Molly M
loy, Cherry Valance, are dillies
names that indicate a Breughel t
who creates a little world of
own, outfitted in every inch v
picturesque hats, insensitive swag
and good-natured snobberies.

Howard Hawks is a bravado s
cialist who always makes pictu
about a Group. Fast dialogue, qui
costumes, the way a telephone
answered, everything is held
gether by his weird Mother I
instinct. The whole population
Scarface, cavemen in quilted sm
ing jackets, are like the first
mals struggling out of the slime
murk towards fresh air. *Only Ang*
a White Cargo melodrama tha
often intricately silly, has a far
unit living at the Dutchman's, a cc
bination bar, restaurant, room
house and airport run by a bene
lent Santa Claus (some airline:
planes take off right next to the
chen, and some kitchen: a pl
crashes, the wreck is cleared and
pilot buried in the time it takes th
to cook a steak; and the chief con
is a crazy mascot who lives wit
pet donkey and serves as a look
atop a buzzard-and-blizzard infes
mountain as sharp as a shark's too
The wonderfully dour reporters
Friday, the mawkish cowboys in
River, are also strangely pinned
place by the idea of people be
linked together in tight therape
groups, the creations of a man v
is as divorced from modern *angs*
Fats Waller, whose whole movie-m
ing system seems a secret preoccu
tion with linking, a connections b
ness involving people, plots,
eight-inch hat brims.

The Mother Hubbard spirit g
the film a kind of romance tha
somewhat Wasp-ish with a Gat
elegance and cool. Both the girls
Scarface, like Zelda Fitzgerald, wo
fling themselves away over a R
Columbo recording of "Poor But
fly." Ann Dvorak, dancing with
big, bland-faced clod who is be
dered by all her passion and he
jerky cat's meow stuff, is so close
Tender Is the Night in her aura
silly recklessness. The sophom

r Gallery.

r the oppressively "hot" can-
 or the mild, peachy ones of
h there are several in the new
. This particular work is most-
eep, alga-green, with purplish
brownish colors. Knowing that
t has actually begun with pud-
of paint, it is fine for him to re-
o a pool's dappled surface and
ous depths. That image isn't
ssarily literal, but it isn't bad,
r, if he intended it.

is exceedingly unfortunate that
t has chosen to show several
    vertical canvases that one
gly suspects were cropped from
r ones(not that it matters), be-
e these works betray a horribly
dy and licentious streak in him.
 are saleable as hand-dyed up-
ery fabrics are, but no more val-
e. There are other paintings,
e that merely parody "compe-
painting," some that may not
ntirely satisfactory, but are defi-
y not dismissible either.

— JANE LIVINGSTON

Become a
legend

hattan for the Indians with his
eyes), or Peppard (unfulfilled,
tly sedentary) playing the ace
ctive role, but playing it less
nically and with much more de-
The real juice of the films is their
giness, that they give you a lot,
zest for what a city contains,
the flatness.
hese movies work partly because
are exploiting the fairly un-
nbed field of 'pessimistic observ-
rather than action, or, for that
ter, acting of the traditional or
hod variety. The work often goes
done, as when Bullitt is shown
ing up and McQueen, trying for
ent-over feeling, does a St. Vitus
ce while suggesting a wave of
sea spreading across his face.
in a long, near-silent and very
d stretch in U.C. Hospital, which
almost excessive in the way it
ks like plaster to the mundaneness
the place, the movie hits into
ut seventeen verities: faces look-
out as though across the great
de of 20th-century lousiness.
hese movies use Hollywood bod-
in a new way which could be
ed city physical: unglamorous, a
of self-contempt (although I don't
Jean Seberg as anything shy of
placency), naturalness empha-
d or pushed to the front of the
en without losing its ordinariness
h Peppard and McQueen have
t rooted-to-the-earth stances).
boy rapist in *Pendulum*, the
ng cop who gets shot in the being of *Bullit,* Lee Remick (too
and too frail for a nympho), Don
ud's very ungraceful, unused to
ning in *Coogan's Bluff*—all these
rs seem to work towards an
l of anonymity through a kind of
eighted gesture and great stretch-
f silent resistance to the material
nd them. There's nothing better
these films than Peppard rifling
yellow pages for the telephone
ber of his wife's beauty parlor,
McQueen eating a sandwich and
king a glass of milk, very tense
guilty about having lost his prize
d to a pair of hired killers.
he scripts are written with the
of a taxi driver, his head filled
routes, the difficulty of getting
ugh crowds, and the cold, con-
ng congestion to be expected at
monument, terminal, or bed-
m. These are not stingy films. If

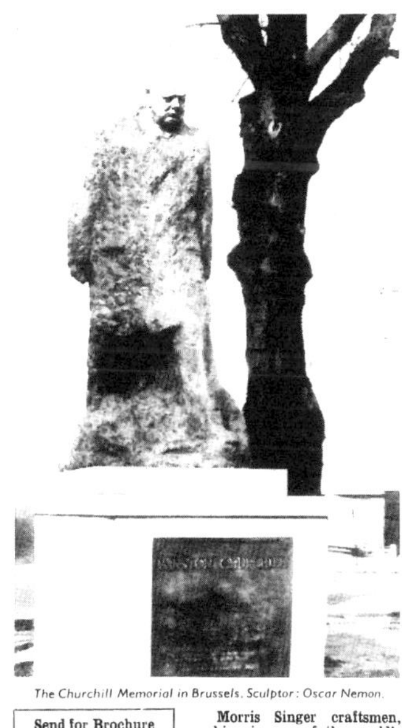

The Churchill Memorial in Brussels. Sculptor: Oscar Nemon.

SK: By doing an illustrated lie for a magazine in my interview with Cindy Nemser, I felt that I had done my job as an artist to present a believable fiction. I was making thousands of pieces of pottery to support myself when I was a student, and I had decided to try to give one pot character and depth that it didn't really have — that I did not have, but that the story created for the piece. I felt that it was archetypical as a Conceptual piece.

(previous 4 spreads) Stephen Kaltenbach, advertisements in *Artforum*, *Smoke* (October 1969), *Trip.* (November 1969), *Teach Art* (September 1969), *You are me.* (December 1969), *Start a rumor* (March 1969), *Perpetrate a hoax* (April 1969), *Tell a lie* (February 1969), *Become a legend* (Summer 1969), *Build a reputation* (May 1969), Courtesy *Artforum*

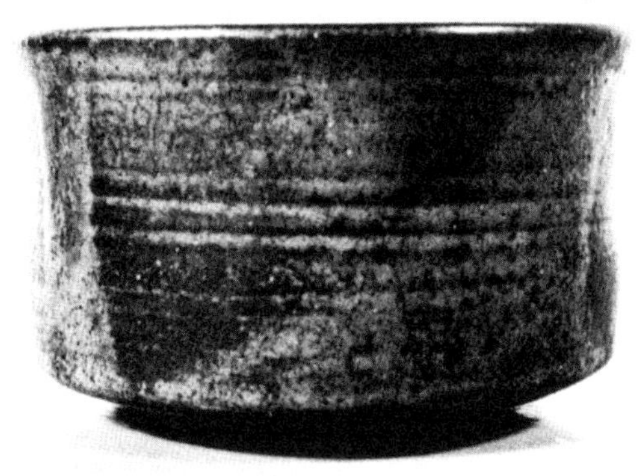

Stephen Kaltenbach, *Ashglaze Pot (Containing Ashes from 2nd Toe of Right Foot of Artist.)*

of the Loom stocking post
pretty chick with a very sho
Right up high on her thigh
"Fruit of the Loom." So wh
I carried the stamp in my
I'd come on one of those
stamp right beside it.

Just working with graffiti
ing about the reaction to art
as art work. So much of e
what we read into it. You s
terms from your own poin
can be anything. We make
use it and we apply it. It re
we apply it to. It's a matter
and who comes to see it y
one in a position of identif
what you're doing become:

That, in a nutshell, explains what I was thinking about at the time. I was thinking that this is not really unlike what novelists do. Stephen King, actually in his book *On Writing*, came right out and said, "Look, we're liars. Everything we're telling you that you're reading now is not true. We both know it, so hopefully, it's not a hurtful thing, but that's what's happening." I was thinking, *OK, as an artist, I can create fictional stuff.* Fictional stuff really has as much existence as a Richard Serra 30-ton slab.

*Fiction may indeed weigh a ton, but one difference —
among many — between King and Kaltenbach is that
the former was and remains up front, so to speak, in his
untruths.*

(above) *Artforum*, November 1970
From *An Interview with Stephen Kaltenbach*, Courtesy *Artforum*

Kaltenbach's first mature New York paintings were intentionally marginal.

SK: People were always talking about what good painting was, and which artists were doing good painting. What makes painting good? It seemed like it not only needed to be good in terms of basic concept and handling, but it needed to be good in terms of the right subject matter. Then what makes painting bad? I decided that the guarantee of bad painting would be a misunderstanding of what fine art was about, a painting that went for complete decoration. A couch painting is a bad painting.

If I were going to enter into painting again through the "Protocol of Opposites," I could do couch painting and be certain that they would be bad in more than one way, because I hadn't painted since junior college. And I knew that ideologically, aesthetically, and conceptually, couch paintings were decorative.

I talked to my friend who worked at Lord & Taylor, who introduced me to a woman who curated the gallery there — they had a gallery in those days. She was very friendly and said, "Sure, I'd love to look at your paintings." I took one month and made paintings that were bad in every way, but I tried to paint them as well as I could. I did nine paintings, the best paintings I could make in a month. I tried to be smart about it because I really wanted to get a show. Eventually, I went uptown to show the curator the paintings. "I don't think you're ready yet," she said. "If you work for another year, come back and see me. I bet I'll be able to give you a show."

JS: They weren't bad enough.

SK: In some ways they were probably too bad, and in other ways they weren't bad enough.

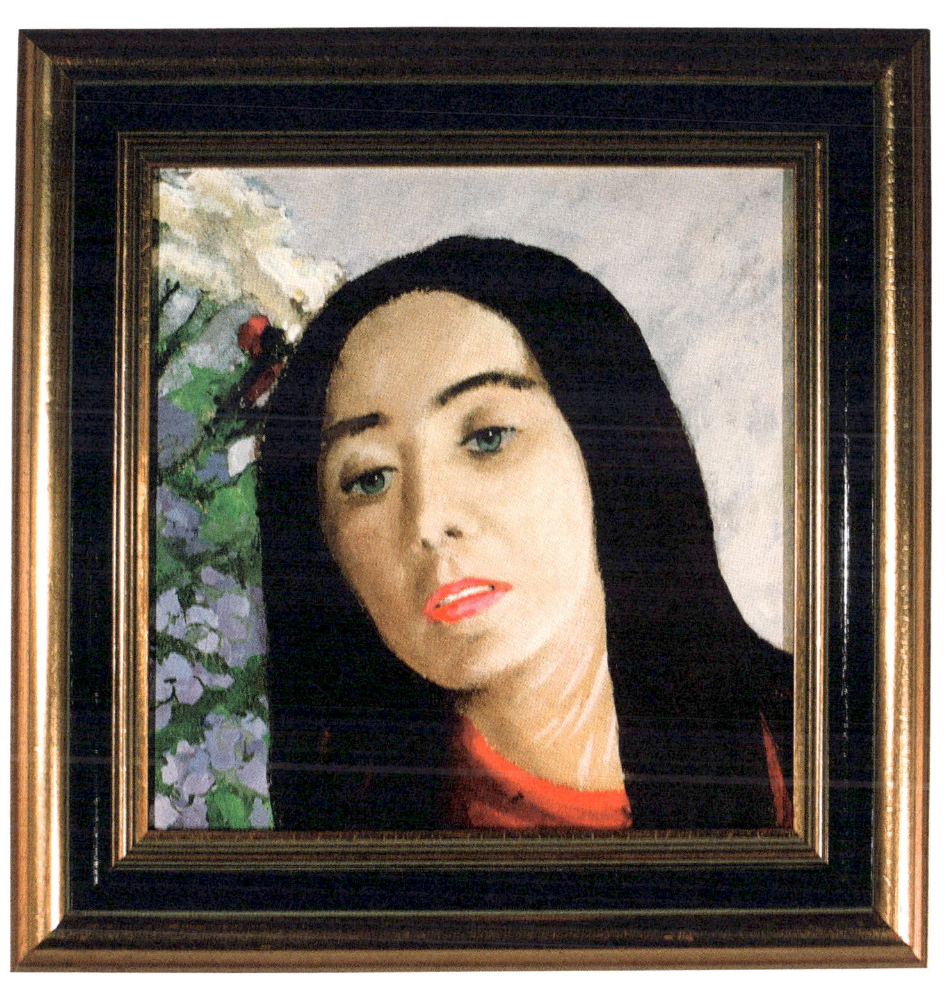

Es Que? (Stephen Kaltenbach), *Silence* (Lord & Taylor Paintings), 1968
Acrylic on canvas, 12 x 9 inches, Collection of the artist
Image courtesy the artist

A recent history of "bad" painting would be gathered in a New Museum exhibition appropriately titled "Bad" Painting in early 1978. Curiously, the show was conceived by curator Marcia Tucker, who organized Kaltenbach's first and only institutional New York exhibition (not of these paintings) at the Whitney Museum in 1969. "The artists whose work will be shown have discarded classical drawing modes in order to present a humorous, often sardonic, intensely personal view of the world," she wrote in the catalogue. "In its disregard for accurate representation and its rejection of conventional attitudes about art, 'bad' painting is at once funny and moving, and often scandalous in its scorn for the standards of good taste."

Figurative and amateurish, Kaltenbach's work could easily be included in such company, but context is king in the world of art, and such artwork would hardly be read as parody on department store walls. Perversely, this is what most interested him about the potential opportunity: Unlike the New Museum, it's a stretch to list a Lord & Taylor show on a respectable CV. Regardless, the exhibition didn't happen.

SK: Anyway, I brought the paintings with me to California. I was storing all my stuff in my classroom, and I showed them to my students, who wanted to borrow them. I thought about it and liked that I could actually put these things out into the world. By the end of the day I had one left, the smallest one; I wanted to keep one because I wanted to have an original as a record. I knew I would never see them again, and I haven't. Nobody has contacted me saying, "Oh, by the way, about that painting from 1971 …"

I'm less unknown than I was when I arrived in New York, but

still, not really well-known. They're in jeopardy to some degree. I have no idea where any of them are. I think that it gives an opportunity for them to go through a sort of natural cycle. I don't know how well-known I will become; it could be that I'm already on the way down and just don't know it yet, or I'm on the way up and just have to die. I would love to see them on *Antiques Roadshow* or something.

JS: Time will tell!

SK: I guess so. There are also all these secondary issues that affect how your work is thought of. I photographed all these paintings. I was an untrained photographer using a borrowed camera, but I had the camera for two years while I was in New York, and I did take a lot of photographs. I got better and better at it. Sometimes my photographs are pretty bad. Sometimes they're actually quite good. Strangely enough, I recently made scans of the pictures I made at the time, and they're great. They're maybe the best photographs I've ever taken.

> *We discussed sales only a handful of times; while inclusion in esteemed exhibitions came easily, financial success did not.*

SK: The issue was that nobody bought anything. And if the works were going to survive, I'd have to take care of them, and I failed. I had a crate, maybe 3 by 3 by 5 feet or maybe 4 by 4 by 6 feet, when I moved out of my loft in New York back to California. It was so heavy that I had movers take it to my girlfriend's basement in Scarsdale [New York]. After a decade the basement flooded, and her dad had everything hauled to the dump. I'm much better at taking care of my own work now.

Despite the anti-capitalistic impulses (at least nomi-cally or aspirationally) at play in much of the artwork of the time, many Minimal and Conceptual artists and artworks became subject to the same blinding forces and demands of capitalism as the previous generation of Abstract Expressionists. Where antiquated forms of brandedness, such as physical signatures or manner of brushstroke application fell off (think "Pollock" or "Rothko"), new forms of identifiable, marketable prop-erties took hold: Lawrence Weiner had a sans serif font, Vito Acconci a sinister vibe, Agnes Martin had lines, and Eva Hesse a malleable and potentially toxic materi-ality. Sol LeWitt had cubes, and Daniel Buren stripes. Hanne Darboven had that incredible scrawl.

Kaltenbach's interest in various fictions addresses a broader question in line with the "Protocol": With so much authorizing going around, especially by critics and dealers, how then might an artist deauthorize their work?

At the time, "a Kaltenbach" might have signaled a mischievous, relatively austere, and nearly anonymous thing or non-thing. But there really was no such thing as "a Kaltenbach." Maybe the artist saw the writing on the wall and got out before it was too late. In the midst of so many contradictions, Kaltenbach may have experienced something of a crossroads. Down one path, the further establishment of "Stephen Kaltenbach" as a look, feel, and — possibly, sadly, and with any luck — as a brand, with potentially exciting yet predictable consequences. Down another, well, something else, maybe even some-thing else entirely.

SK: I was visiting my parents and photographing my dad fairly often. They lived in Berkeley, so I was driving down from Davis at the time, in 1974.

He hadn't spoken a word to me in a year or two, or to anybody else, as far as I knew. The last thing he'd said to me, he was looking up at the ceiling, where there was a very cheap glass fixture over the light bulb. It was square with bunches of grapes that were frosted on the inside. He pointed up and said, "Fruit bowl." I remember thinking, *Wow, he said two actual words, and I understand what he's thinking.*

A year and a half later, I'm sitting there with him, and he looks over and says, "I have to get up and go to work." *Wow, he said a complete sentence.* Of course, he wasn't going to get up and go anywhere, but that didn't matter to me. "When I get there, I'll try to contact … I will contact you." At that point, I was sort of speechless, and then he said, "I'll be able to because the boss will let me. The boss is a great guy. Don't ever work for anybody else."

JS: Do you think that what your father said that day was somehow a precursor or premonition to your encounters with God?

SK: It sure seems like it. I could say I believe in God, and I do, but I think it would be more accurate to say that I think that the experiences I've had can't be explained any other way. If I look at my life, it all seems to be evolving in harmony — poetically, linguistically, and experientially.

Anyway, I think my dad lived for three or four years without exercise before he died at the very end of 1974. When it happened, the whole family was around for Christmas. My brother had driven up to Sacramento in his camper van and was staying in my driveway overnight. Before he left in the morning, I got the call from my mom. It was the last day of the year.

We all headed back to Berkeley and had a private funeral in the living room. I said, "We could just start by saying all the great things about our dad." He was a special guy, a very, very loving, self-sacrificing person, and we all felt the same way about him.

My sister Mary, who was Dad's favorite, started freaking out and trying to talk and wasn't able to. She said, "I'm seeing him."

JS: Had she had visions before?

SK: Yes. She's very quiet about it normally, but I wasn't surprised. Not at all. I come from a family that goes way back into my great-greats with stories of supernatural experience. By the way, this is why taking LSD didn't slow things down at all for me.

Many years before that, my mom told me that she had come in one day and my grandmother was crying, and that God had told her that she was going to die soon. She would go out in the woods and meditate at night and come back talking about hearing the engines of the universe chugging away.

His language really picks up in passages like this, and displays a familiarity with the immaterial and mysterious that far precedes (and exceeds) his time in graduate school or New York.

So my mom said to my sister, "Tell me what he's saying." Dad told my mother through my sister that he appreciated everything Mom had done.

My younger brother, John, was house-sitting in the Berkeley Hills and suggested we go up there and pray all night. He was a Christian at the time, and I was a Zen Buddhist. I was in another bedroom, and I was just — I don't know if you're familiar with Zen meditation, but, well, you have a cushion and you sit. If you're alone, a good way to do it is to face a featureless wall. You don't have your eyes shut, but you're not looking at any specific thing.

He said, "I'll pray, and you can do your zazen, and we'll just do it all night long." We had an amazing experience, staying awake all night praying. I was in the same spot from approximately 9 p.m. until about 4 a.m., when I suddenly had a vision, and it was kind of funny: It was a pile of pirate treasure.

It looked about two or two and a half feet high, just a dump of coins and cut gems on the floor. Maybe six or eight feet in diameter. It was like if you took a whole lifetime of booty and dumped it out. It was a pirate thing because there were a couple of swords stuck into the pile. One of them had a necklace dangling from the hilt, thrown over and hanging down. It was brilliantly lit with amazing detail. As I remember, it was all cool colors, and there was no gold; it was all silver. Highly reflective.

I don't know if my mouth was hanging open, but it probably was; it was certainly worthy of that. All of a sudden, I heard my dad's voice, and it sounded like it used to when I was a kid. He had a very loud voice if he needed it to be loud, and a very good speaking voice. Part of his job was speaking to groups of farmers, actually.

What I heard was "Too much. Toooooo much." He was more adamant the second time. "Toooooo much."

I'm sitting there looking at this pirate treasure, goods stolen from sunken ships with murdered victims. It was easy to interpret when I put it that way. I suddenly realized I needed to get rid of everything. I had a house full of stuff in Sacramento — this was at 51st and V Street. It was a little modern place with a storefront next to it, a former five-and-dime I was using as a studio. I actually had the canvas for Dad's painting stretched in there, and it was too small of a place to work on it. The ceiling wasn't tall enough to light it evenly, and I couldn't get back far enough from it to see the whole painting. I had a plant collection, an antique toy collection, an art collection, and a furniture collection. Living there was taking a certain amount of effort and attention; it seemed like I was carrying a physical, philosophical, and psychological burden in having all this stuff, so I got rid of it all. I was perfectly comfortable with everything being gone, except the canvas, which I stored with the stretcher at school; it was a big office.

I moved to a place in Davis with just a bedroom, a little desk, and a single mattress on the floor. I had four roommates, and the five of us made amateur music together at night, playing instruments and singing. It was terrific. From there I seriously started looking for a place to make the painting.

THE BARN

SK: One of my roommates, Julie Partansky, later became the mayor of Davis. She was a very good friend and a great musician. She had a friend who had a boyfriend who lived on this ranch out in the country. It turned out he lived next to the barn.

He explained to the owners, the Jarretts, that I was doing a very big painting and needed a big space with a big wall to work on, with adequate viewing distance. Their barn was 40 feet long, and opposite the painting wall were these two big barn doors that swung open so I could get back a hundred feet to look at it when I needed to.

I had an interview with the Jarretts' son before moving in. When I met him for the first time, he was wearing a hard hat and trying to be as menacing as possible, but he had a twinkle in his eye. Anyway, I guess he decided that I was normal enough to have on the ranch, so I began my move out there.

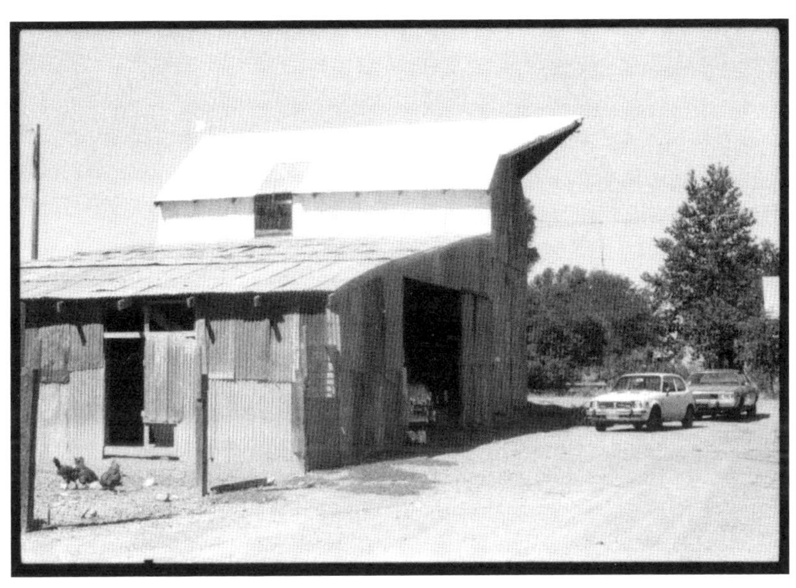

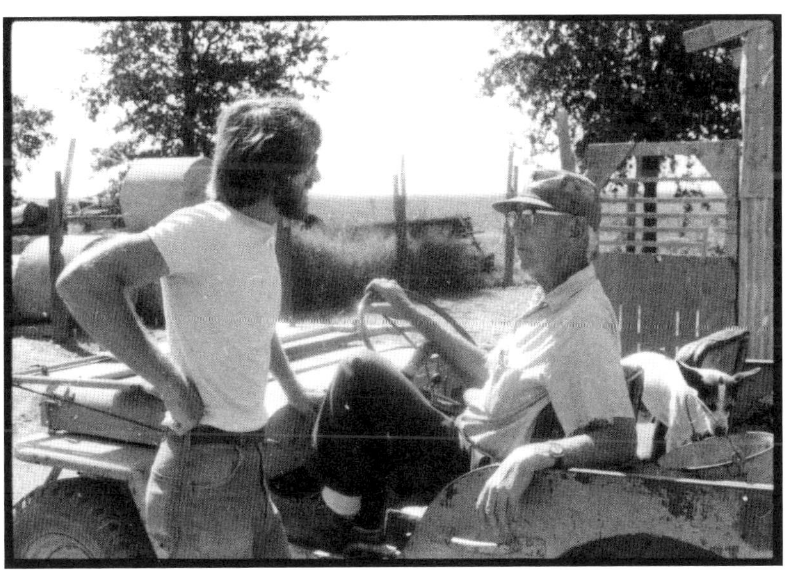

(top) The barn, 1970s, Photographer unknown
(bottom) Kaltenbach and Mr. Jarrett, 1970s, Photographer unknown
Courtesy Oakland Museum of California

Just five years earlier, and in stark contrast to securing the barn lease, Kaltenbach had arrived in New York, where he was quickly centered within a radical and blooming social and artistic scene. Writer Roger White notes that Kaltenbach asked a taxi driver to take him where the artists live. Apparently a man standing at the corner of Spring and Greene took one look at the young import and asked if he needed a loft.

I prepared the barn, which was just a corrugated metal structure with 18-foot walls on one side of the road, and the ranch house, which was from the 1880s, on the other. I was able to put a bank of lights very high up so I had terrific light to work under. I remember that I didn't insulate it at all, I just stapled heavy-duty plastic to the walls and ceiling and poured concrete on the floor. I put in electricity and water, and that was it. That's how I lived.

I was somewhat isolated out there, and it wasn't easy to visit as I didn't really have an address. I liked not having an address. I felt that it was advantageous to me to have a rather unwelcoming environment because I needed privacy. There was no bathroom, so it meant that the visits didn't extend too long either.

When I lived in New York, I was a very social person. When I was living in the barn, I was not that social. Out toward the end of the painting, that broke down more and more as people visited and we talked about what I'd been doing. I was surprised that living in such an unwelcoming place didn't help more to maintain privacy. I really loved the pursuit of process. I loved the fact that I would run into challenging situations but that there was always a solution to whatever the problem was. A conceptual connection with the present moment is so important when making art, and it's so hard when you're not alone, and so, I mean, the solitude, it can be a very important thing.

I'd turned away from contemporary, Conceptual, and Minimal stuff, even thinking that what I was doing might not only fail, but might cause me to be forgotten. I remember thinking that was something we couldn't know. In a way it's not up to us. When I'm ready to start a new project, it's like a home invasion. It forces itself into my consciousness, and there it is, and I have to deal with it.

This striking sentiment tracks with most artists I know.

I became rather close with the farmer and his wife, who lived in the ranch house. I must have gone to 20 or 40 Sunday breakfasts at their place. Other than that, I wasn't involved with food that much. I ate either very simply or rather poorly when I lived there. I would sometimes drive into Woodland to get fast food; my diet improved so much when I got married, oh, goodness. I had stuff out there, but really simple stuff, cereal or fruit.

JS: How did the Jarretts respond when you said you wanted to live in a place with no plumbing or insulation?

SK: I think they were interested in the entertainment value it might provide. They would stop by occasionally, and sometimes their son would come with them. They'd come in and chat, but just for a few minutes. My primary visitor was Mrs. Jarrett. She would bring me my mail, and we'd have a little talk sometimes. She was a very active 80-year-old. She had a heart attack on her front porch when she was 93. She talked to me afterward about it, and she said, "I was lying there on the porch thinking, oh, you know, it was morning, the air was cool, it was beautiful." And she said, "This is such a nice place to die." But she didn't. She lived to be within just a couple of months of 100. They were both very resilient people.

JS: What did the Jarretts charge you for rent?

SK: $25 a month.

JS: And were you teaching in Sacramento at the time?

SK: Yes. It was a 40-minute commute to work, which I did two days a week. I did that commute for 10 years.

JS: When you moved in, did you have any idea how long you'd be there?

SK: I knew that it was going to be a long time. The range of how long I thought it might be was very wide. That level of attention, giving that level of attention to your painting, it's really very fulfilling.

It's not far from the center of Davis to the edges of Davis, an area largely defined by its partitioned farmland and university programs in agricultural science and veterinary medicine. Kaltenbach's metal barn, surrounded by some of the most arable land in the state, stood more than 10 miles west of town and about 30 miles from his Sacramento State classroom. A nearby highway spur, Interstate 505, connects two major freeways, where the crops of California's Central Valley travel east-west from the Bay Area to New Jersey, and north-south to Mexico and Canada. To the west, the Vaca Mountains mark the valley's edge. The barn sat across a straight, quiet road from the Jarretts' simple white house; the next nearest was almost a mile away.

It's hard to square that his barn — at the crossroads of State Road 92D and an irrigation canal — was just two hours from the literal intersection of Haight and Ashbury, and that his time in the country overlapped with such significant changes in the city, like the rise of punk, wane of hippie-hood, kidnapping of Patty Hearst, assassination of Harvey Milk, and the 1974 move of Jim Jones's Peoples Temple to Guyana (not to mention their tragic ending in 1978). And that was just San Francisco history.

Like other seekers from coast to coast, Kaltenbach fulfilled his generational promise of turning on, tuning in, and dropping out, forging a wholly new path, one complete with visions dark and illuminating. It was a back-to-the-land-ish movement of one, when to go alone was perhaps to go further.

JS: You don't have to answer this, but how did you go to the bathroom?

SK: Well, I guess I might as well go into detail. There was a lot of area around the barn that was like, the history of agricultural machinery: piles of moldering, rusting, sinking-into-the-earth agricultural machinery. It was a very complex area with trees, and my barn was surrounded by all that. I used a posthole digger — basically, a tool that digs a round hole as deep as you want — I would dig a round hole in an area where nobody walked. It was blocked off by either junk or trees or chicken wire and other stuff dumped all over the place. I would have a hole and a pile of dirt that I took out of the hole.

I was buying these little paper bags in bulk, and I would do my business ... Am I being clear enough without being too gross?

JS: I read you.

SK: ... in a paper bag, fold it up, and then I would take it out and drop it in the hole down six feet or something. I'd put a little bit of dirt on top. The hole was like eight inches wide. It was covered up with dirt, buried, and it was ready for the next one, which usually happens, hopefully, the next day. It's not that bad a system, really. I'm not sure that the trees benefited from the fertilizer, but anyway, that's how that worked, and it was pretty easy.

THE EDGE

In moving to the barn, perhaps Kaltenbach further reconnected with his dad on a workaday level, and in a sense even reported to him over the course of the painting's production. Or maybe it was simply in line with a lifelong habit of charting the unknown.

SK: At the age of six months, my mom was changing me on her bed — about four feet off the floor — and she turned to pick up a clean diaper. I charged off the edge, launched myself into space, and landed on my nose, which has been crooked ever since. I think that's a good metaphor for how I lived my life for many years.

My father worked for an insurance company as a field supervisor for Michigan and the surrounding states. He had an airplane and flew from state to state to all the field offices. He was also an animal enthusiast. We had an 80-acre property in Michigan with springer spaniel hunting dogs, goats, and chickens. At one point, we had hundreds of chickens. The bunch got smaller and smaller until finally, by the time I was in high school, we ended up with just a horse and cow.

We moved to Indiana and then Washington, Oregon, and

California, where the family got bigger and bigger and poorer and poorer. He eventually became a secretary of the Contra Costa County Farm Bureau, a big farmers' organization that had headquarters in every county, and he was commuting a lot, home just on weekends.

When he got a job in Sonoma County as the secretary of the Sonoma County Farm Bureau, we moved just outside the town of Sebastopol. We were very, very poor. I remember he was earning $237 a month and supporting a big family, but things were cheap in 1952. When we were at our most financially desperate, my mom went back to work, so my grandmother took care of us when I was about 10 years old. My mom wanted to have 12 children, but she stopped at seven. Most of them were in Berkeley throughout the '60s and '70s. My sister Mary was basically a little mother taking care of all of us because the family kept growing.

I often wish I wasn't such an independent kid. Instead of hanging out with my grandmother and my sister, I was mostly out trying to set the forest on fire. We did some scary things, like collecting pine pitch and making torches with tuna fish cans nailed to the ends. We filled them with pitch and lit them on fire — good fuel. It burned like crazy, and we'd go running around the forest. It's amazing we never set the entire state on fire.

IRRITANT

I went to school at Santa Rosa Junior College, where I was taught by Robert Arneson. I was his first student who wasn't still in high school, and we hit it off immediately. I don't think you can teach artists unless you're willing to be open about what's going on with you; I feel like it's almost a requirement to be honest and open. You can't teach the good stuff. You can show people how to do stuff, but that's about it.

SK: One time I was with Bob as he was sculpting the eyes of a portrait. He did one eye and then he drilled a perfect hole for the other. He said, "I decided that I needed an irritant." The idea of doing something wrong became very, very important to me and spread out in all directions of my work. There was a seed planted that day in Bob's studio.

I took a class with the painter Maurice Lapp, who encouraged me to continue and recommended UC Davis to get my degree.

I was in the Naval Reserve and was drafted to active duty, so for two years I was on a troop transport ship which spent most of its time on the Pacific Ocean going between San Francisco and Japan.

When I got out, a moderate drinking problem I'd developed came with me. I was tired of working for peanuts, so I applied for a job with the Santa Rosa Fire Department. A certain amount of athleticism was required, and my physical was planned for a Monday. The Friday before, which was Friday the 13th of July, 1962, I got drunk on my motorcycle and smashed my foot, making myself forever ineligible to be a fireman. I remember lying in the hospital for six weeks; I'd turned my foot around backwards. I was looking at it, thinking, *this is the luckiest thing that's ever happened to me.*

I went back to UC Davis for graduate school, and when I got there, I felt no inspiration for painting and decided to shift to 3D — ceramics and sculpture. My first year I had critics come into my studio who asked me to explain what I was doing. I began to feel that I needed to have something to say. As art students at Davis, we were expected to be able to talk about our work, and in order to talk about our work, we needed to be thinking about things. It was no longer just get an idea of a visual presentation of some kind and then make it. It had to have a story. This requirement seems to have continued to grow over the years. I loved the idea of making something that not only had value in its poetic content, but also in its development of philosophical ideas.

JS: You seem to value spontaneity and intuition as much as rigid conceptual processes and methodologies.

SK: That's very true. That kind of intuitive and spontaneous dependence for the source of your vision seems to generate interesting conceptual stuff. That was certainly the case with Bruce Nauman.

JS: You overlapped?

SK: Yes. He changed everything for a lot of people, including some of the UC Davis faculty. It seemed that every day he was experimenting with new ideas. Bruce was a good friend all through school. He came into the program doing these small pieces that were OK, but not all that interesting: Plexiglas, pierced circular holes mounted over mirrors, diamond-shaped framed pieces, one by one foot. But right away he started trying new things; he welded up a bunch of steel pieces and painted them with really thick oil paint. A couple of weeks later, he threw it all away and started building fiberglass objects that rested on the floor and leaned against the wall.

He did a plaque to be screwed onto the trunk of a tree, and the bark is supposed to slowly grow over and cover it up. The plaque said, "A ROSE HAS NO TEETH."

As Kaltenbach notes, Nauman's plaque was intended to be attached to and eventually swallowed by a tree. And it was attached, at least on several occasions (there appear to be more than one fabricated), though I'm not aware that any tree has fully metabolized the object.

One such plaque was at some point removed from its native habitat and formally accessioned by a museum, where it was documented in uniform, artificial light (opposite, top).

By contrast, another image (opposite, bottom) was taken by Tony May, Nauman's friend from their under-graduate days in Madison, Wisconsin. Nauman gifted May a copy of the plaque in the late 1960s, one made of Bondo, a resin-based filler, which was affixed to a tree in front of May's home. It, too, has since been detached, sold by its owner years later to support his family.

SK: By the time I was in graduate school at Davis, students fought over ideas. It was a part of the dynamic. One afternoon I was in another artist's studio. "How're you doing?" I asked. She was making sculptures out of fiberglass and resin.

"I'm bored," she said. "These two materials are just so common, and I'm not feeling very inspired."

I was looking at some little sketches on the wall, and she had this small watercolor; it looked like figures under a blanket. The figures

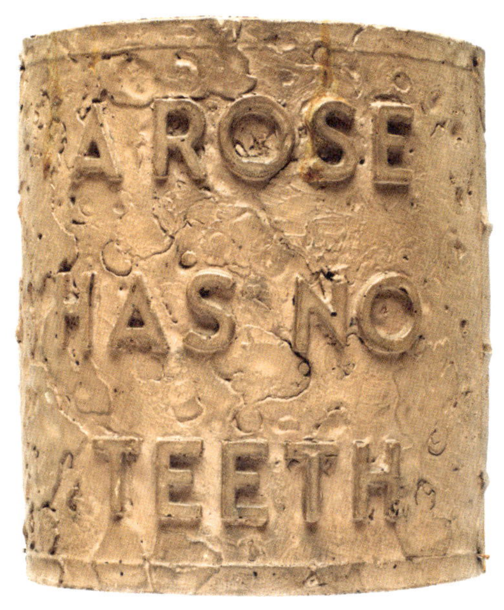

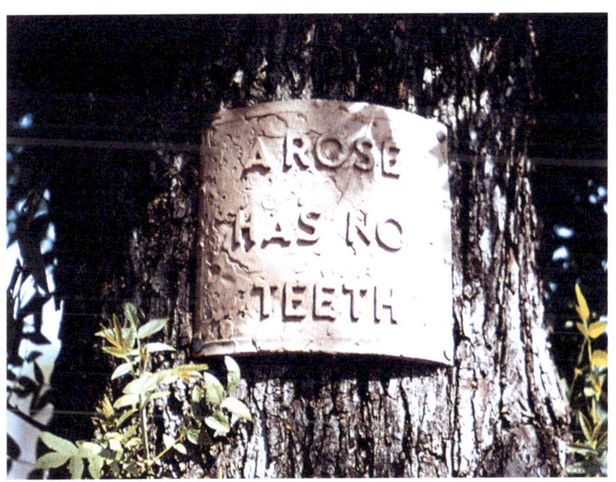

(top) Bruce Nauman, *A rose has no teeth*, 1966, Polyester resin, 7 3/8 × 6 3/4 × 2 3/4 inches, San Francisco Museum of Modern Art, Gift of Pat and Bill Wilson, © Bruce Nauman / Artists Rights Society (ARS), New York, Photo: Katherine Du Tiel; (bottom) Image courtesy Tony May

97

were brown, and the blanket was green. So I said, "Well, this looks like dirt and grass. You could be working with those materials."

Anyway, I got very excited, and I immediately did a couple of drawings, my first drawings of earthworks. I came back to the seminar the next day that was run by Bill Wiley, and she showed up. We put all our stuff up, she came over and said, "Hey, that's my idea."

And I said, "I didn't realize I gave you sole possession of it."

The best thing is that *Artforum* came out, I don't know when, but it seemed soon after, and there was this turf ring sculpture on the cover by a great Conceptualist, I mean Minimalist Conceptualist, I can't remember his name. He did big, hanging, felt works.

JS: Robert Morris?

SK: Yes, there you go. I'm losing my mind.

> *It's curious that while Morris was a central part of his New York story, his name slipped Kaltenbach's mind here. That said, it wasn't necessarily Morris whom he intended to name.*

It was really amazing, because here this student and I are, having this little tiff about whose idea it was, and then Robert Morris, this giant guy in New York doing this big thing in Germany. His piece was so — I don't know if you've ever seen an image of that, but it's so beautiful. My goodness. What a nice work. Anyway, it was also an illustration of how ideas run throughout the cult of contemporary art.

Morris' work was indeed featured on the cover of Artforum, but not until September of 1974, and not with an earthwork, but with a detail of Labyrinth, a sculpture made from Masonite and wood. In any event, Kaltenbach finished school at UC Davis in 1967.

He may be thinking of Michael Heizer's Isolated Mass/Circumflex, a Nevada earthwork that appeared on the cover in December 1969. If so, his recollection is a conflation: Kaltenbach's advertisements in Artforum culminated with the rather heavy declaration "You are me" the very same month Heizer was on the cover.

Another "ring" artwork appeared on the front of the magazine between Morris and Heizer: Richard Serra's To Encircle Base Plate Hexagram, Right Angles Inverted, a half-buried piece of metal on a dead-end street in the Bronx and his first outdoor installation, in March of 1971.

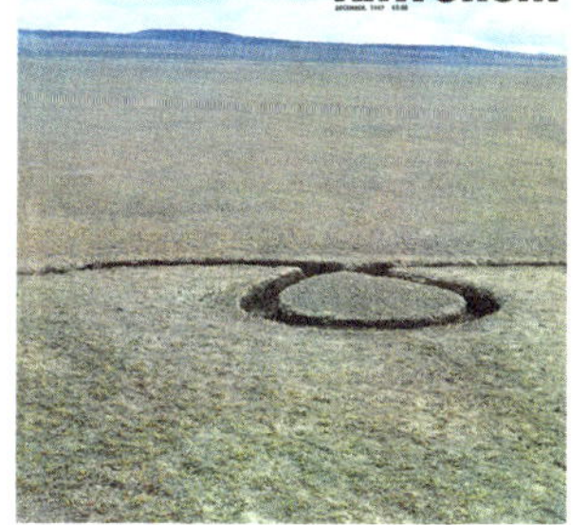
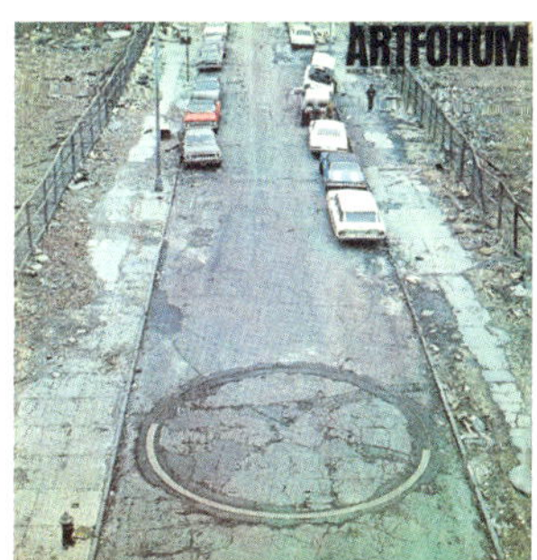
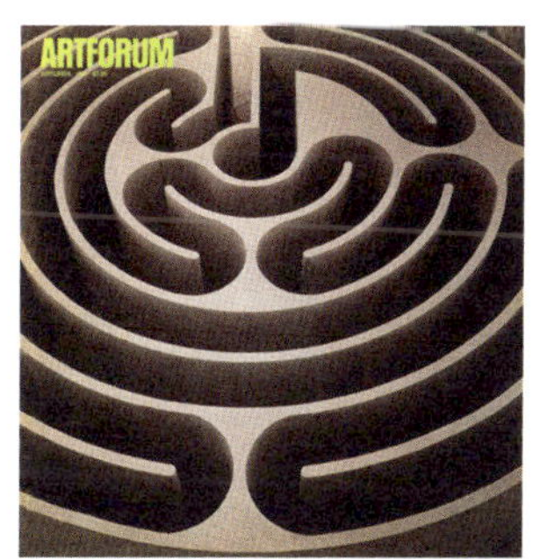

Artforum covers: December 1969, March 1971, September 1974
Courtesy *Artforum*

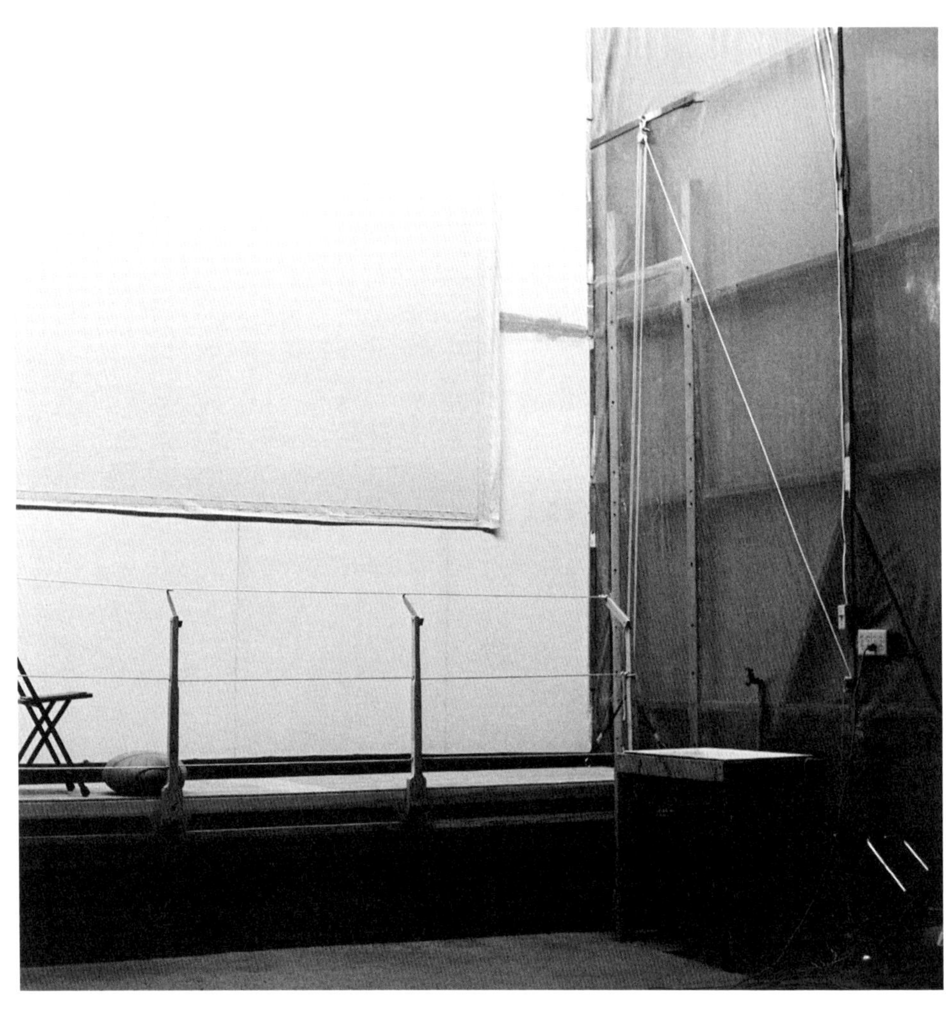

Stephen Kaltenbach, *Portrait of My Father* in progress, 1970s
Photographer unknown, Image courtesy the artist

JS: How did the painting of your father begin?

SK: I got all set up and projected the photograph onto the canvas, and I went home — at that point, I had just moved into the barn, and so there was a transitional period from where I rented a room in the house with friends in Davis. I'd put plastic over all the walls, and I sealed up the two barn doors, but there was a big crack, and the north wind came up, and the plastic became like a sail. I had the opaque projector up about as far as I could reach, and the plastic pushed it over and totaled it.

I thought, *uh-oh, maybe I shouldn't use a projector.* So I gridded off the painting and the photograph. And what I did was stretch the canvas directly on the wall. There was no stretcher. I just put in nails and stretched the strings really tight across. That worked as a grid. I had an equivalent grid with an ink line on the photograph, and so that's how I transferred the image.

JS: How big was the original source photograph?

SK: It was 18 by 24 inches, mounted on card stock in black and white. It was quite strong but ended up getting pretty battered over the years because I would bring it everywhere with me.

I was friends with Roger Vail, a photography professor, and I was able to check out a 4-by-5-inch camera, which probably was a mistake because I think the exposure was wrong, and so the quality of the photograph was not wonderful. There was also the focus problem, which made the hairs seem wider than they were.

At a certain point, I think about halfway into the project, I decided to visit my dad's younger brother, Herman, in Ohio, and take some photographs of him.

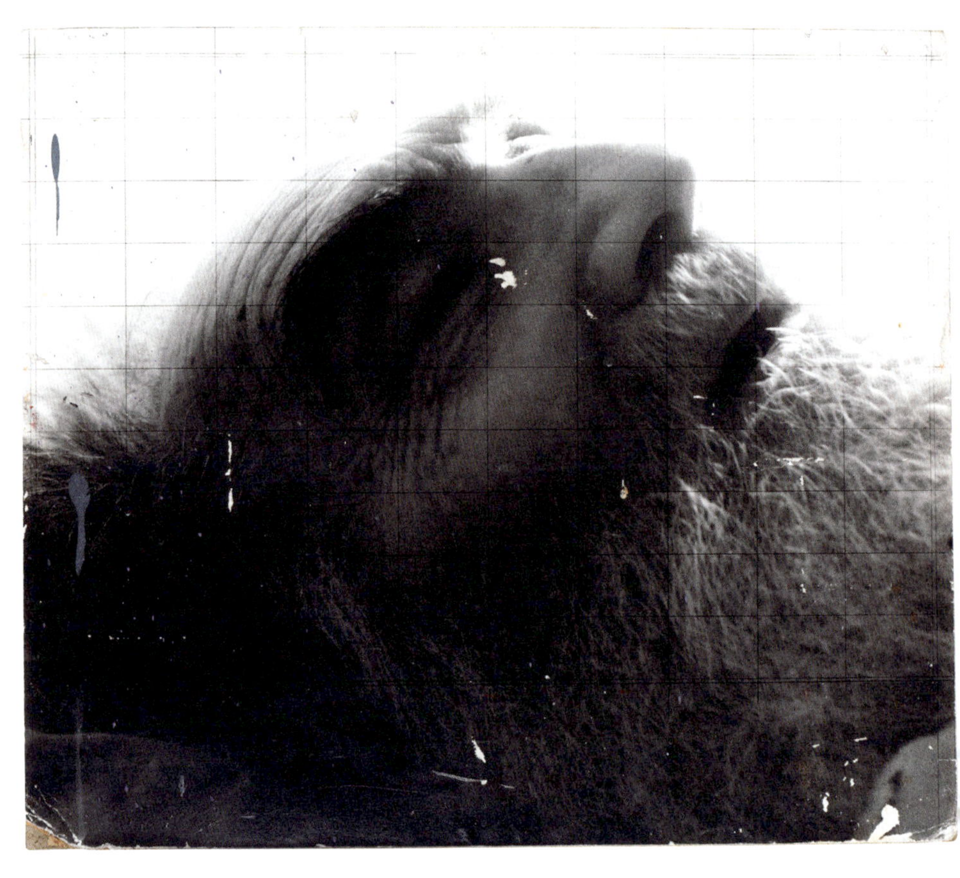

Stephen Kaltenbach, *Portrait of My Father* source photograph
(Wayne Kaltenbach), early 1970s, Collection of the artist

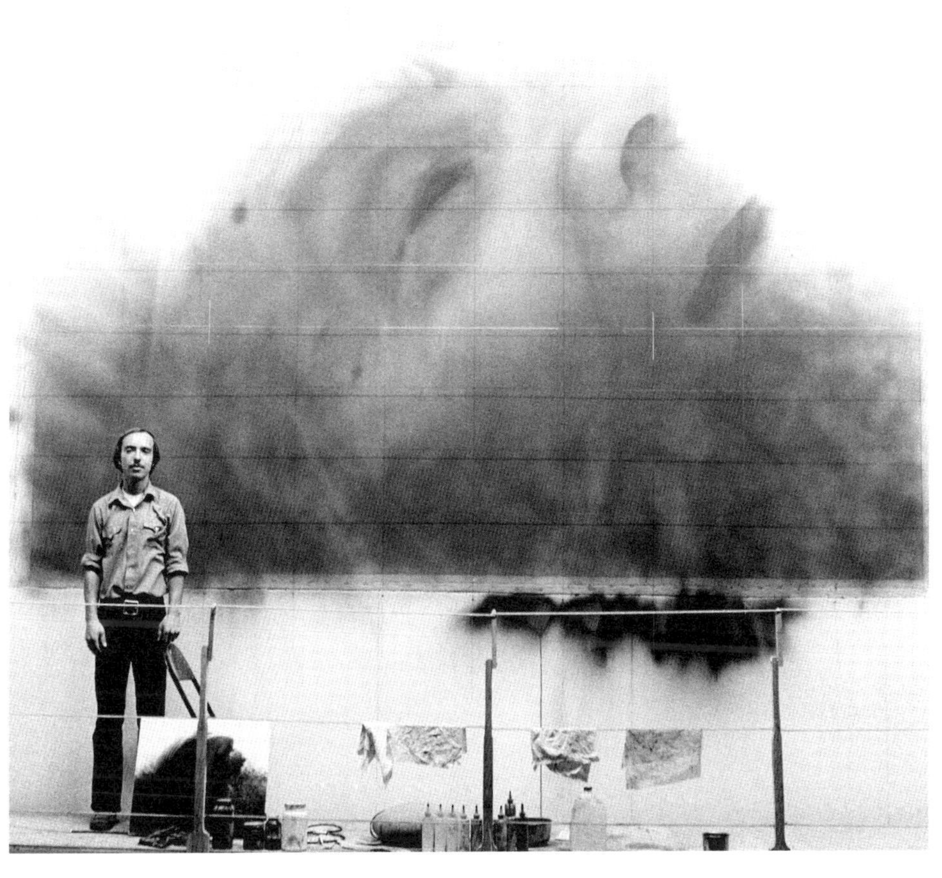

Stephen Kaltenbach, *Portrait of My Father* in progress, with former student, 1970s, Photographer unknown, Image courtesy the artist

JS: What did he think about that?

SK: Well, he didn't tell me until after, but posing as his dead brother, well, that was a sobering experience for him. [laughs] I really could hardly believe I had the gall to do it. Good grief.

I did use those photographs to some degree. He doesn't look all that much like my dad, but he did have a beard and mustache, and the hairs. Beard hair is beard hair. It worked for me.

JS: But when you're painting that many beard hairs, you're not really painting individual beard hairs. So how did you do it, or think about it?

SK: Good question. If you look at the trees that Grandma Moses paints, for example, and then you look at the best realist landscape painters, well, two things … one is that they're different. It's pretty much Grandma Moses's painting, what Grandma Moses knows about a tree, rather than what she sees when she looks at a tree. A realist painter paints what they see when they look at a tree, and other things, too. In a way, both artists are also painting what they know about painting. There are aspects that may be convergent and other aspects that are miles apart, but they both end up with valuable expressions.

Grandma Moses (born Anna Mary Robertson Moses in 1860) was a 78-year-old widow in rural Virginia when she began painting cozy scenes of country life, which she sold at local fairs alongside her prize-winning pickles and preserves. Soon after, a collector took note of her work in the window of a pharmacy, and three paintings were included in a Museum of Modern Art exhibition

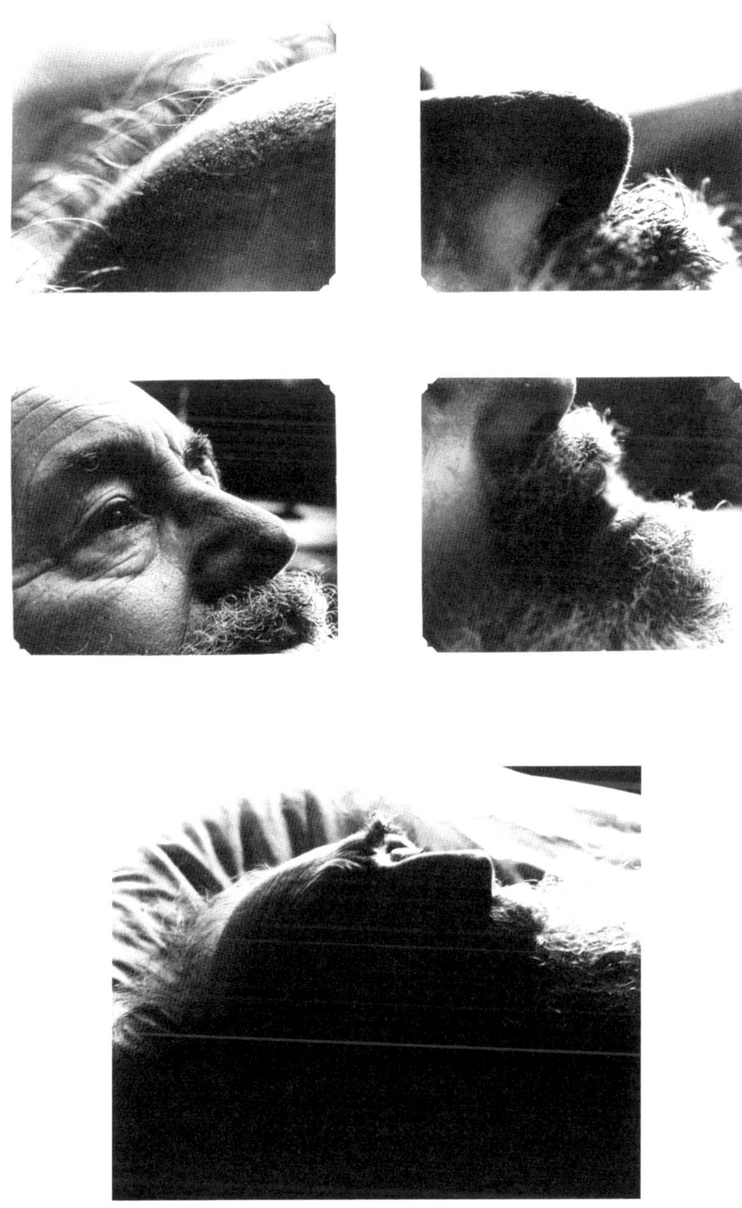

(top) Stephen Kaltenbach, *Portrait of My Father* photographic studies (Herman Kaltenbach), 1970s, Courtesy the artist (bottom) Stephen Kaltenbach, *Portrait of My Father* photographic study (Wayne Kaltenbach), ca.1973, Collection of the artist

called Contemporary Unknown American Painters. *Hallmark purchased the rights to reproduce her paintings on greeting cards, which made her a household name. She died at 101.*

JS: Do you think you painted what you knew about your dad?

SK: I would like to say that, but I think it's a little more basic, a little more fundamental. I was working from a photograph, but the photograph was a little out of focus and underexposed; there's only so much information, and that's why I went back to Ohio and plied my poor uncle for more information. In a way, I think that I was painting the detail in my dad's face a little bit more like Grandma Moses painted trees. I hope that I'm expressing that correctly.

JS: Yes. How did you think about working both in color and black and white at the same time?

SK: I started by painting the portrait with warm colors at the top and cooler colors at the bottom, and I covered the entire thing with patterning, in color, so that the color was contained within the curvilinear vine and leaf elements. Everything that was negative space was black and white, and everything that was positive space was color. That division between black and white and color remains throughout the whole painting, but I didn't even recognize what it was doing visually for some time. I didn't realize what I liked about it, but I knew I liked it.

There's a lot of discrete division between color and black and white. I think it's one of the things that works visually without announcing itself very strongly — it's surprisingly subtle, although it's not subtle at all. You walk up to it and you can just feel it.

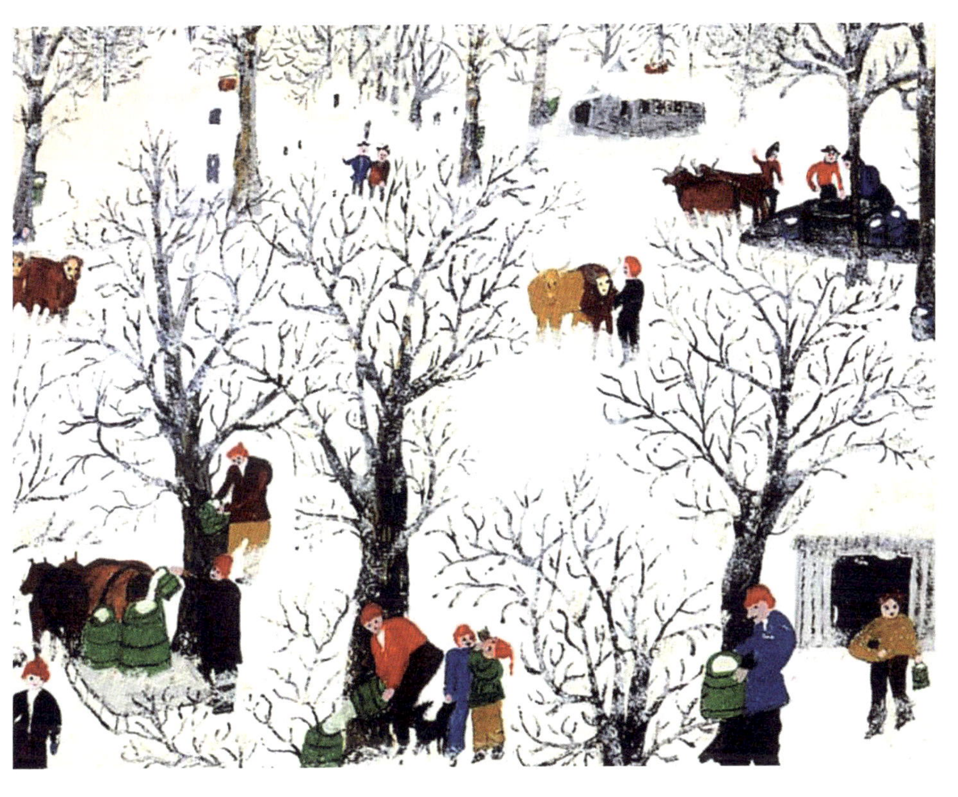

Grandma Moses, *Sugaring Off*, 1943 (detail)

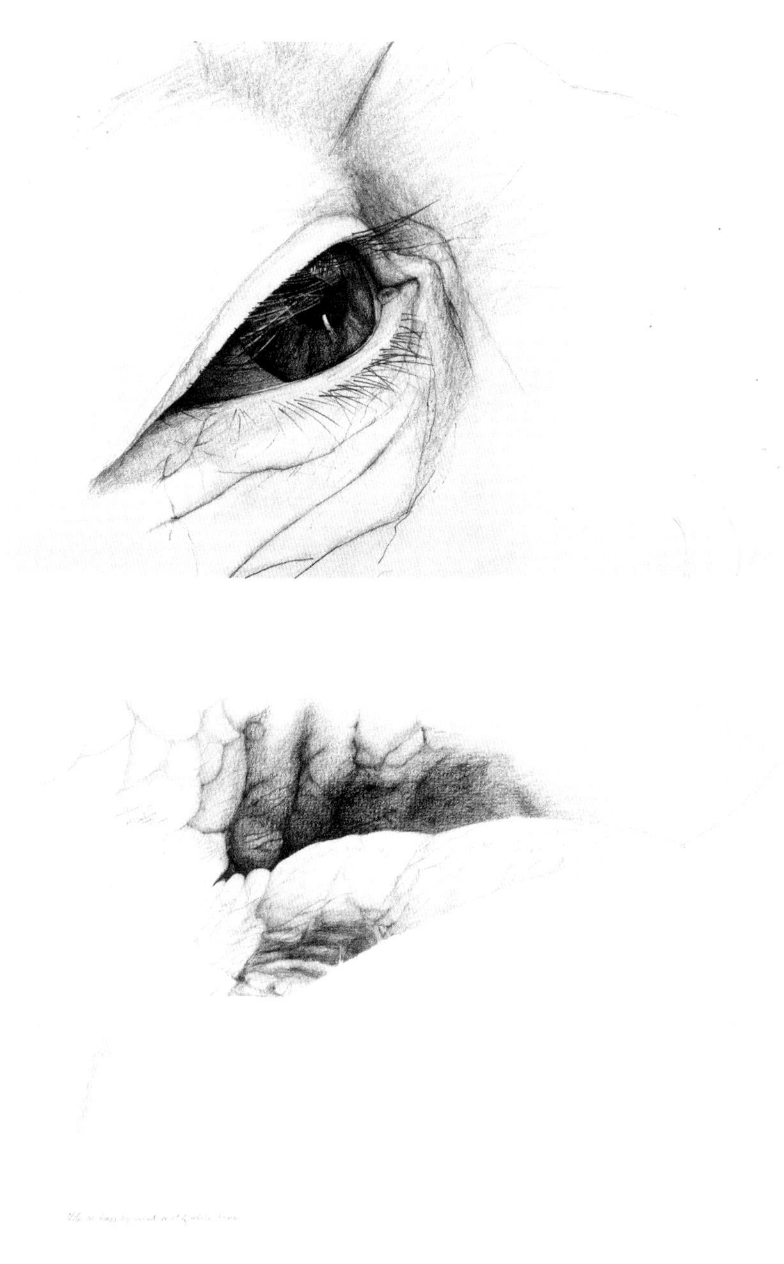

Stephen Kaltenbach, *Portrait of My Father* drawing studies, 1970s
Collection of the artist

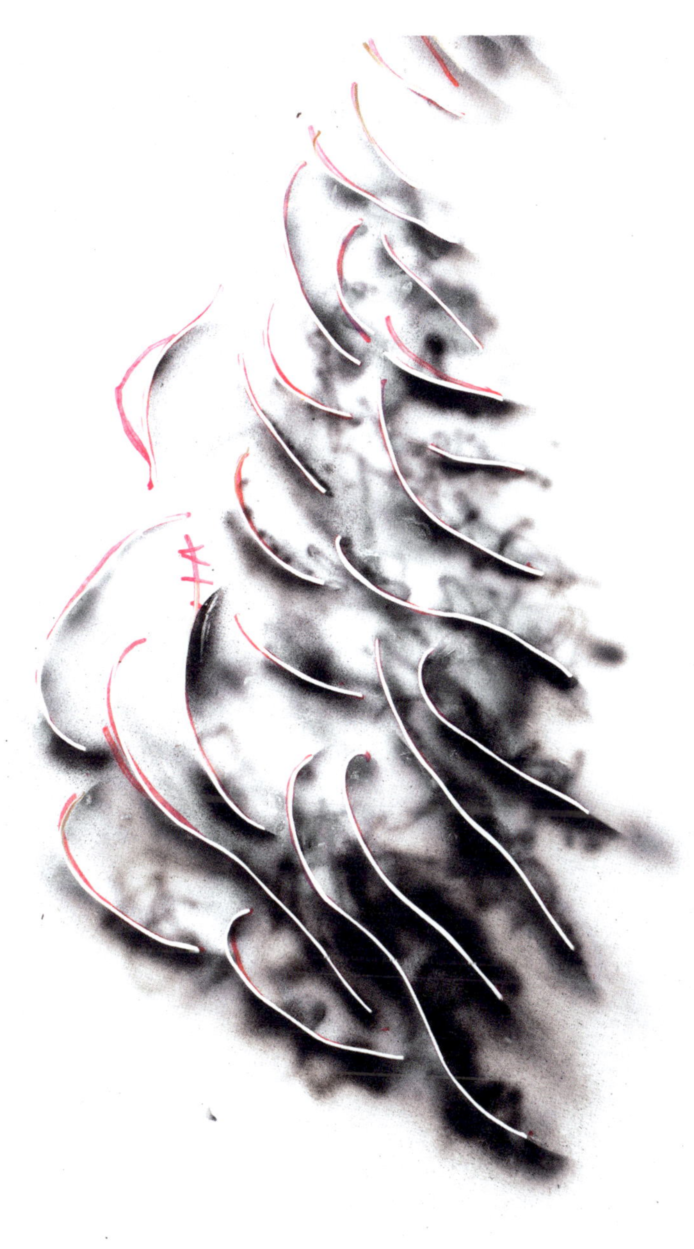

Stephen Kaltenbach, *Portrait of My Father* stencil, 1970s
Collection of the artist

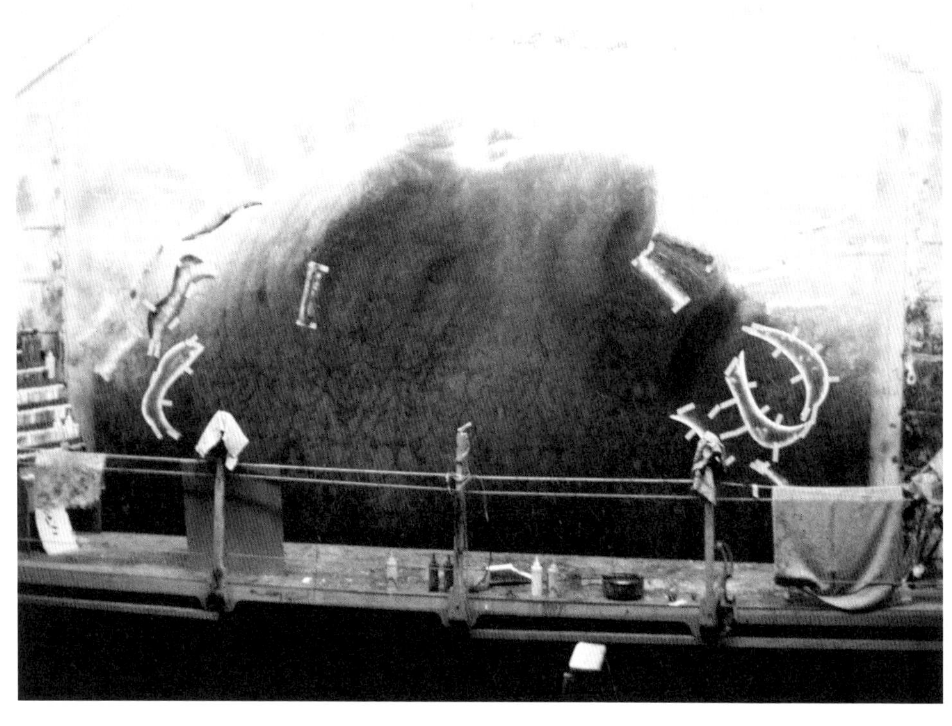

Stephen Kaltenbach, *Portrait of My Father* in progress, 1970s
Photographer unknown, Image courtesy the artist

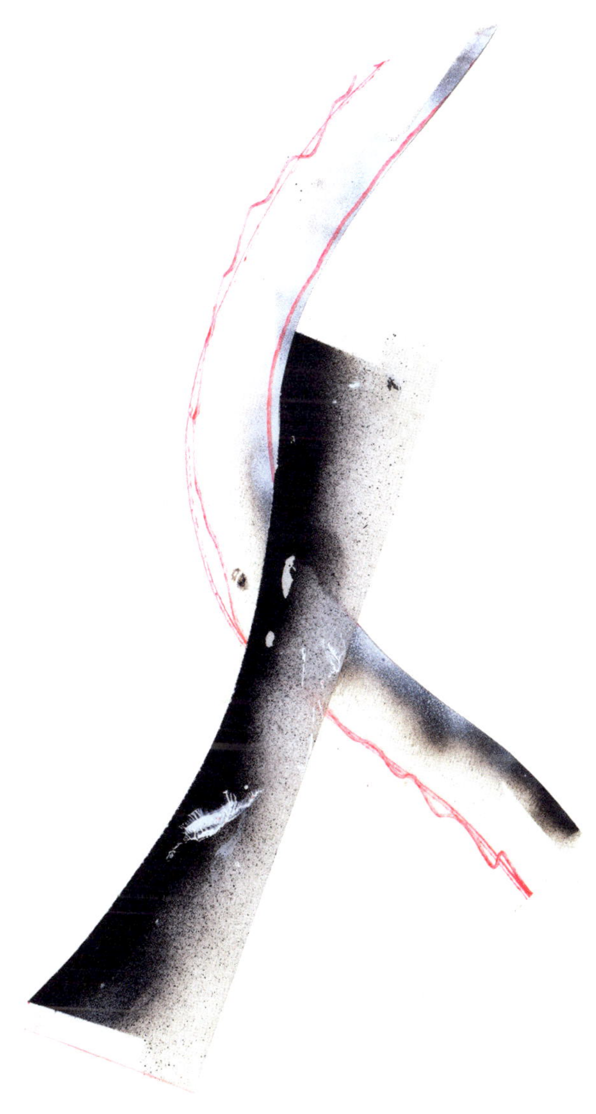

Stephen Kaltenbach, *Portrait of My Father* stencils, 1970s
Collection of the artist

SK: Inspired by Islamic patterns I found in that book in Wisconsin, I drew the pattern I would use for the portrait of Dad. I started that pattern drawing in the late spring of 1970 and finished it that summer. If I spent a whole lifetime just making patterns, well, I don't think there would be anything better.

The pattern that I used with the portrait of Dad is a vine and leaf pattern from Islam. It was constantly shifting, and it was always perfect. It seemed to be able to evolve and transmute, always continuing. The colors were sort of heavenly, I guess I would say; the color harmonies were astonishing.

Kaltenbach developed his pattern from a William Morris example, which was likely derived from Islamic arabesque, a tradition that looks to ornament as anti-image (often with plant tendrils, leaves, and flowers) and connotes the coherence of nature and the wisdom of God. In a religious context, this sort of patterning privileges the spiritual world, submitting that the material world, by contrast, is an imperfect smoke screen of the infinite universe's underlying weave.

Morris was a 19th century English humanist and polymath best known in his lifetime as a poet and posthumously recognized more for his work in textiles and pattern design, including wallpaper and fabrics. He was a founder of the Arts and Crafts movement, an early socialist, and a collector of artworks from the Islamic world.

The influence of Eastern art and culture on Morris is increasingly recognized, and the relationship between his work and Portrait of My Father *is palpable in a number of patterns, including* Flowerpot *(1883) and* Lodden *(1884). According to Róisín Inglesby, curator*

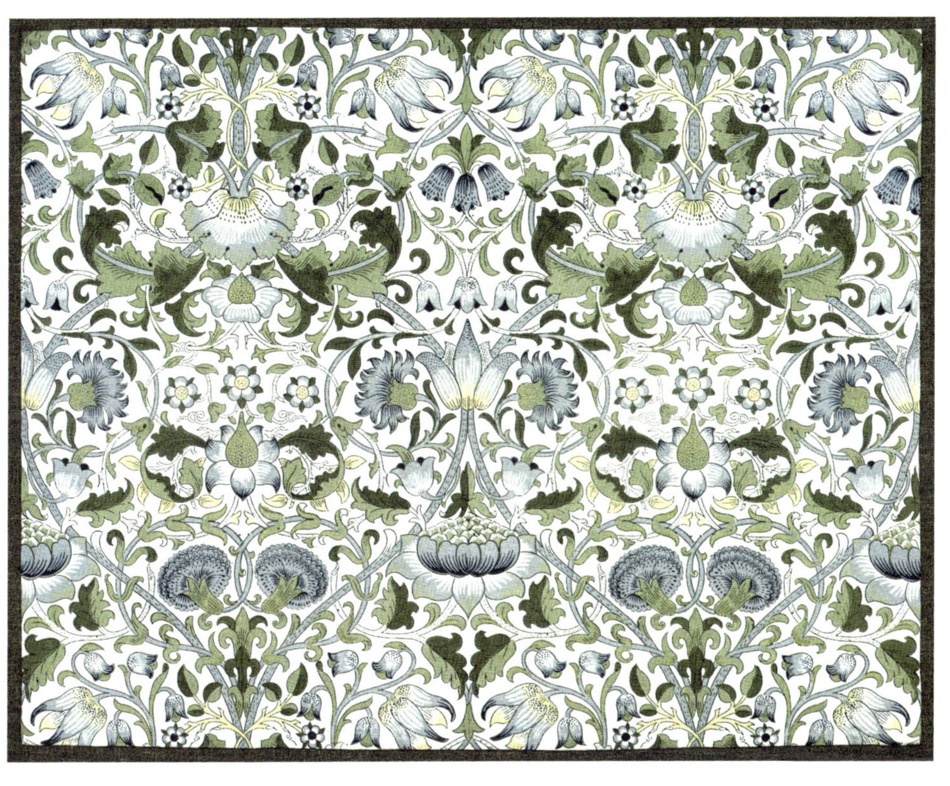

William Morris, *Lodden*, designed 1884, Printed cotton, 73.7 x 97.8 cm. Manufactured by Morris & Co., Image courtesy William Morris Gallery, London Borough of Waltham Forest

I decided I wanted not only to have the pattern be depicted in terms of color against black and white, I wanted it to be depicted as a crystal item.

JS: How did you begin to imagine the pattern as a three-dimen-sional object and actually go about rendering it on the canvas?

SK: Well, I had no idea what to do, and it was not working at all. I had the realization that I had to have really good optical infor-mation. I had to build it. I actually made the vine and leaf pattern out of Plexiglas. I wanted to express the joy of that psychedelic mescaline experience, the pattern and the image.

I glued the drawing of a linear pattern to the Plexiglas then used a band saw to cut the pieces apart, so they were just flat

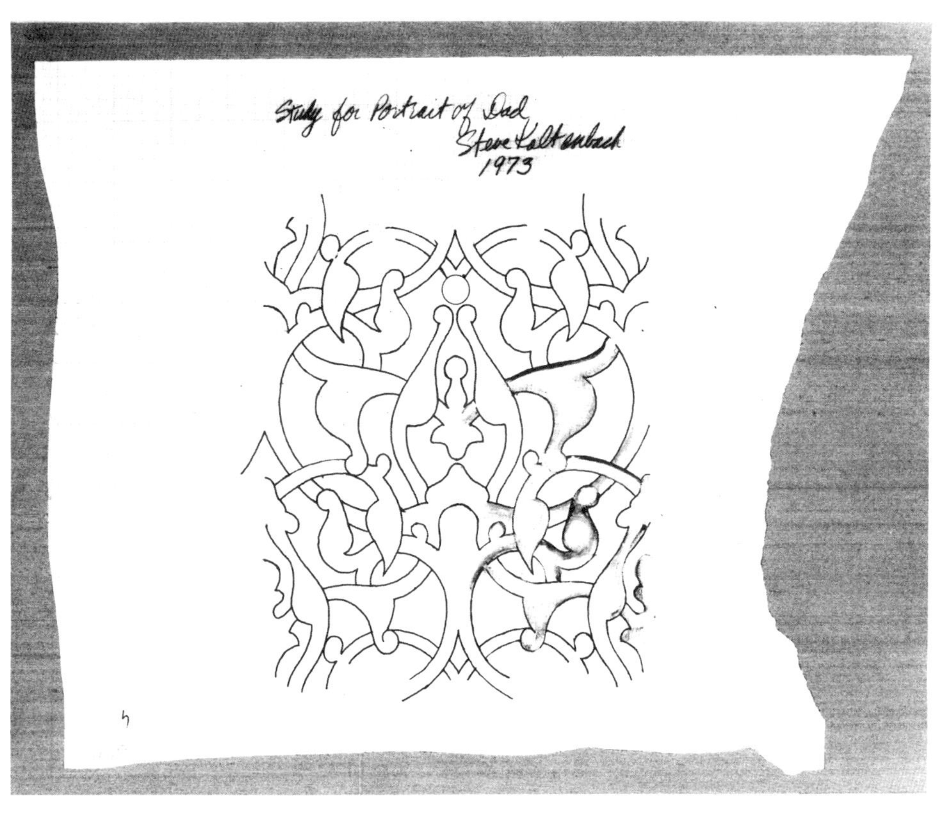

Stephen Kaltenbach, *Study for Portrait of Dad*, 1975, Courtesy the artist

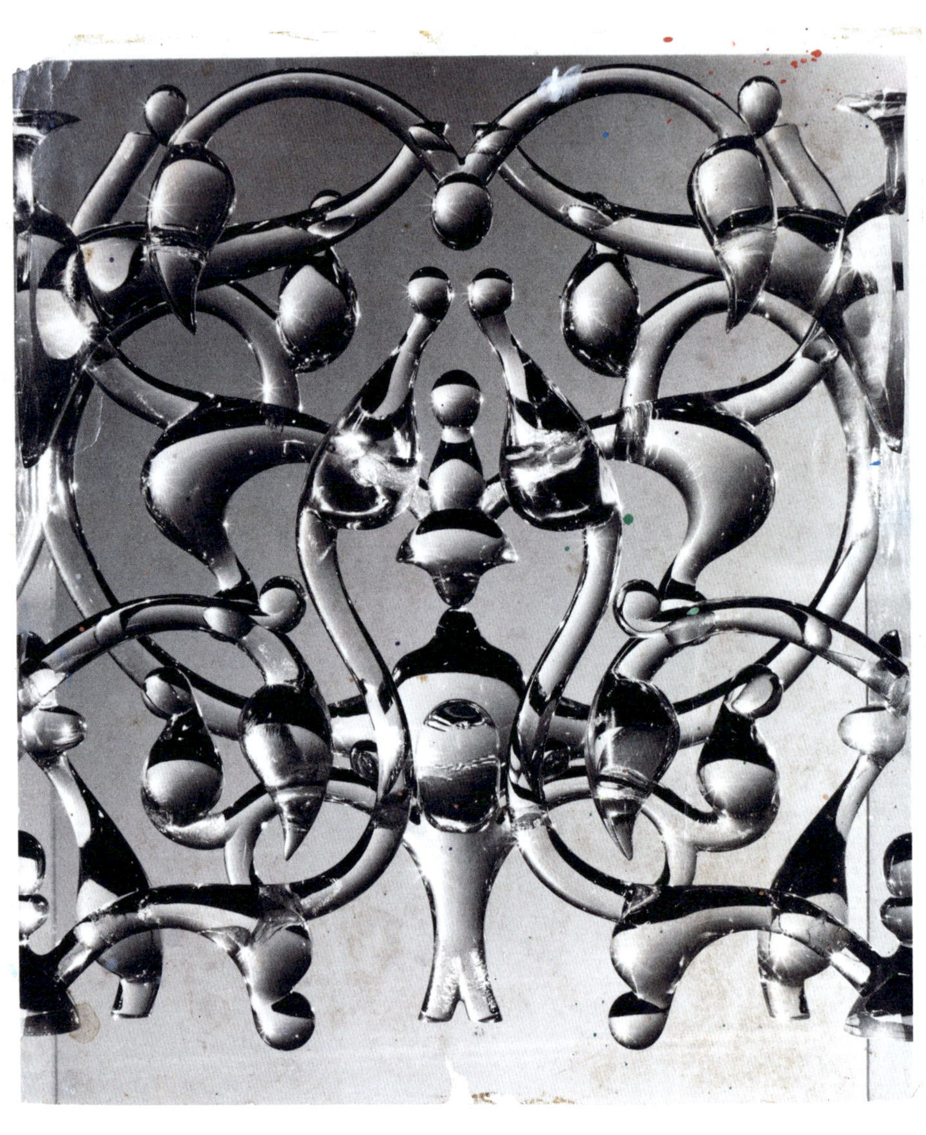

Stephen Kaltenbach, *Portrait of My Father* photographic pattern study, 1970s
Collection of the artist

with square corners. Those had to be thickened in places where the pattern swelled before there were thinner places in the stems and leaves and buds and so on. I used glue and power tools, a belt sander, and I roughed out everything. I started actually making the shapes of these things.

I contacted my mom, and she got the whole family together in Berkeley, all my brothers and sisters. We had a weekend where we had food and visiting. It was really a terrific time, and everybody helped. My brothers and sisters used files and sandpaper and blocks and different things; I worked with them and monitored what they were doing. We actually used toothpaste as a final polish.

I photographed the Plex "still life," as I called it, many times. I was photographing one morning facing the horizon outside my barn when the sun came up and all the polished Plexiglas forms I'd made were little lenses; they contained images that were beyond the still life. Each tendril contained within it an image of the earth and sky that was compressed down to almost a hair's width. Each little lens has a curve, and within that curve is a dark line that represents the earth and a light line that represents the sky compressed to this curvilinear element that was perfect to represent the hair. I still have the remaining part of the stencil. We can hold it up and you can look at these big curving tendrils through the Plexiglas. It was just to visualize what the pattern would look like if it were clear; it was research to see how light would move through the transparency. I had made exactly what I needed, and it happened without me knowing what I needed.

In the spring of 2024, I visited an exhibition of Kaltenbach's pedagogically related work called Teach Art *at Sacramento State, where he taught for more than three decades, engaging students as participants*

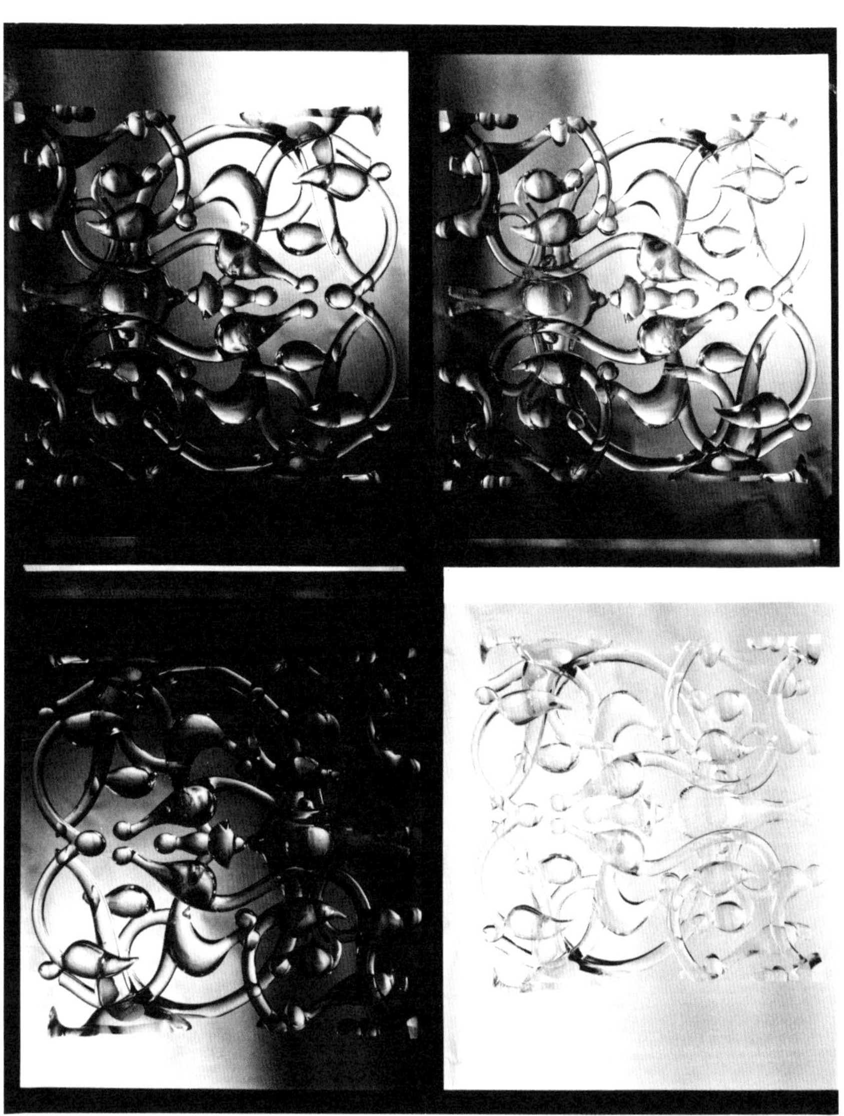

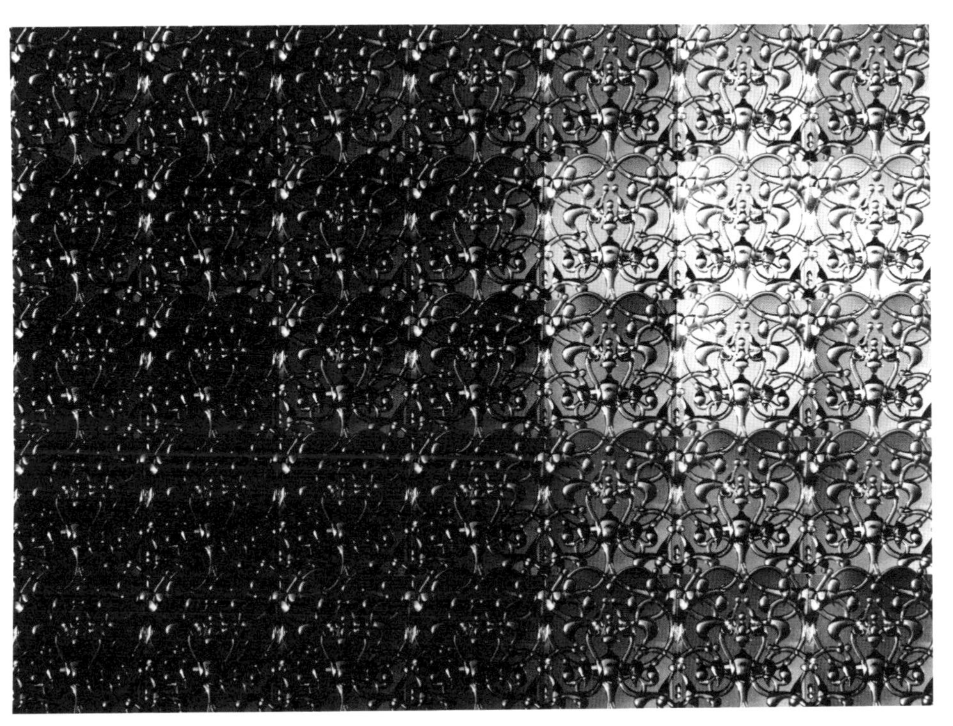

Stephen Kaltenbach, *Portrait of My Father* photographic pattern studies, 1970s, Collection of the artist

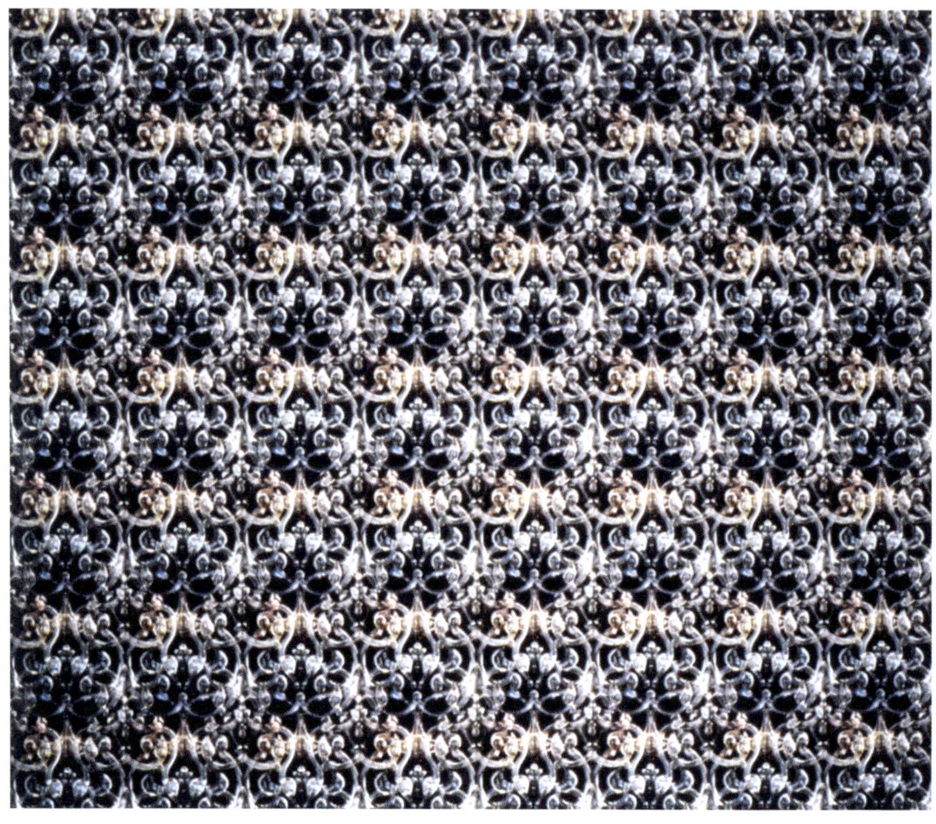

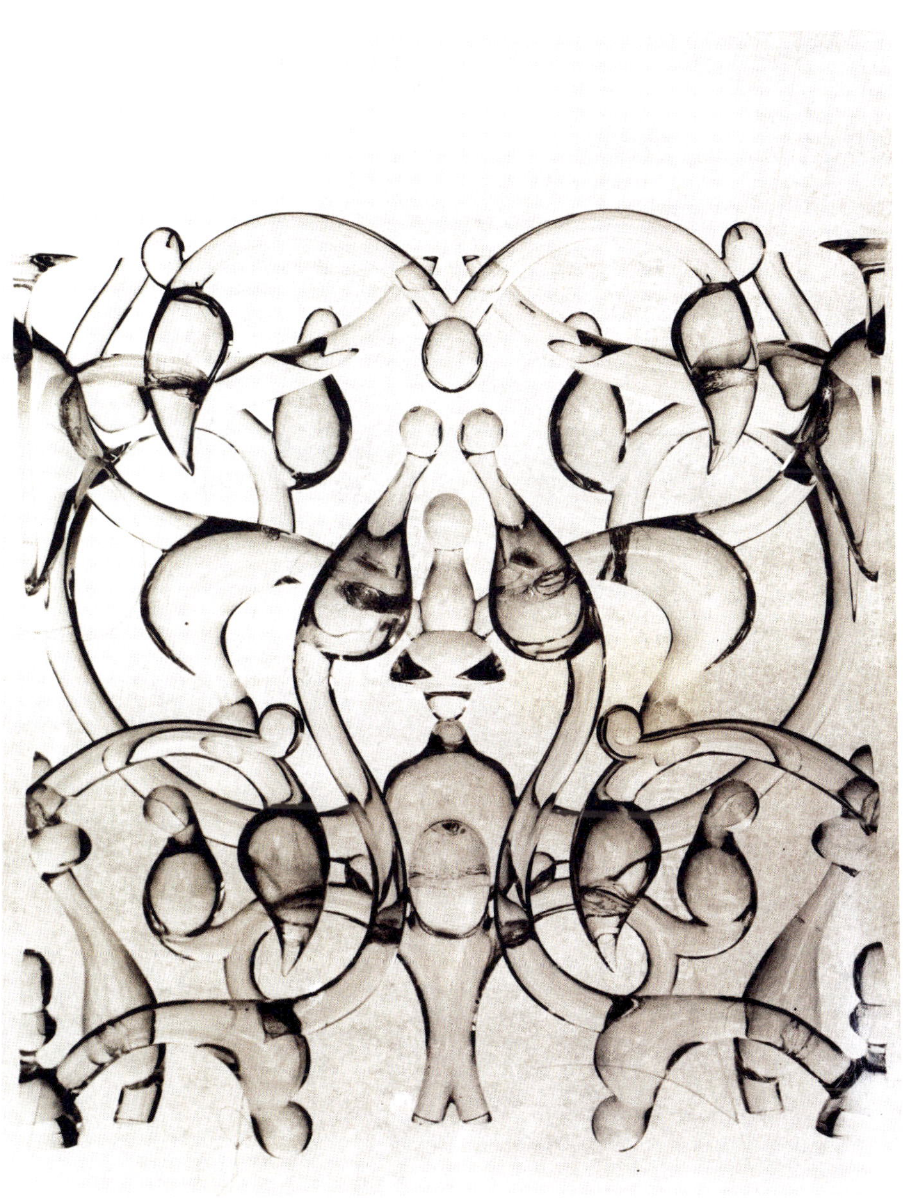

Stephen Kaltenbach, *Portrait of My Father* photographic pattern studies, 1970s, Collection of the artist

and collaborators in various artworks and experiments. Among many other things, the show featured archival materials related to the making of Portrait of My Father *— after all, he commuted from his barn to the classroom — including the surviving piece of Plexiglas stencil. The exhibition's curator, Kelly Lindner, invited me backstage to witness various treasures that she'd unearthed in Kaltenbach's Davis storage locker. I was unaware that such materials existed; in fact, Kaltenbach himself had forgotten that he'd held onto so many* Portrait-*specific photographs, pattern studies, stencils, and more.*

JS: Did you know how to paint? Did you consider yourself a painter?

SK: I was learning as I was doing, so naturally I got into phases when I didn't like what I was seeing. Other painters could have done it better, but I'm not convinced that the work itself would have been more successful if it were better. The level of awkwardness that shows if you look closely gives it a level of abstraction that I find interesting.

I know painters who have a much higher level of skill; it's impressive to watch them work. But it shouldn't only be your visual ability, vision, and dexterity that goes into a painting. I do recognize these things as missing in my own work. It's also my laziness, just how much time I'm willing to spend working instead of goofing off and wasting my time. All those things add up to what goes into the work. It needs a certain, I don't know, if you want to call it magic.

When I painted the first 20 hairs on my dad's cheek, my landlord comes into my studio, and he's standing at the back looking at what I'm doing. I'm up on my platform, and he says, "Are those hairs?" And then he says, "Them things look like broom handles

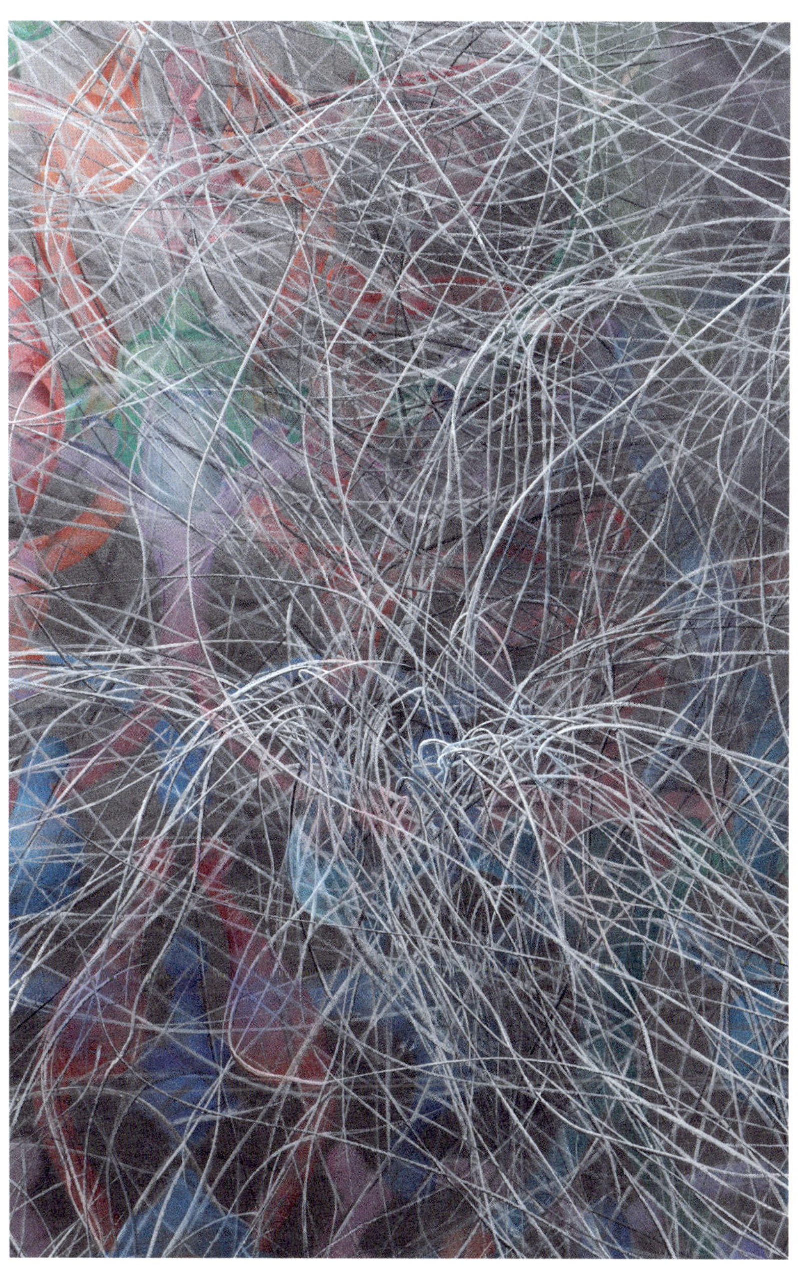

Portrait of My Father (detail)

sticking out of his cheek." I went back and joined him, and indeed they were way too wide and way too flat. But I never changed them — they're still there. They're at the bottom of a network of beard hair, but they're still there, and I like them being there. I don't see those things as diminishing the quality of the work.

There were days when I would work like crazy for 16 hours and only have accomplished 10 hairs. I had this epiphany that at the rate I was going, I would look very much like the painting by the time I was done. In other words, I would be 75. I had to come up with another way to do it.

When I was in high school, I used to do the pinstriping on hot rods using a saber brush. It's a brush that has hairs that are about an inch and a half long, and the handles are very short. It worked amazingly well on the *Portrait*. I was able to dip the brush into two plastic lids: one side in dark gray and the other in light gray or white. Then I went from these 10-hair days to painting hundreds of hairs a day that were much more dimensional and believable.

At first I was dissatisfied with the way the hair looked in the light, until one day I saw a string hanging in the barn. Sunlight was hitting it, and it had a kind of double halo; it looked like it was enveloped. I realized that probably will work. And so I began to do that with some of the hairs that are really lit up.

JS: The light moves through pattern and image fairly seamlessly.

SK: I continued painting back and forth between pattern and image throughout almost the entire process. More and more I was able to do both pattern and image at the same time. In the upper-right-hand corner, I began to paint a secondary pattern and then a fourth and a fifth, simply by using a sample that masked out the existing patterns, so I was only painting within the openings. One aspect of the painting was that there were areas where there was

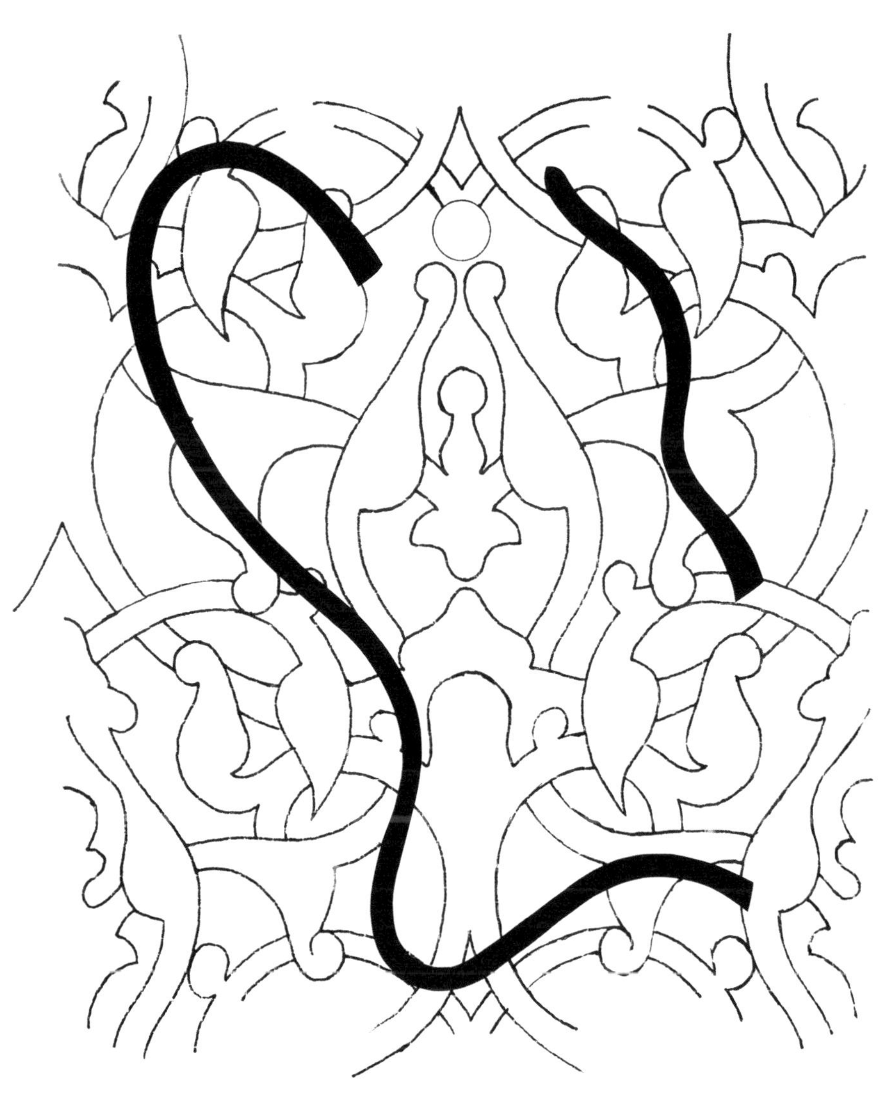

Stephen Kaltenbach, *Portrait of My Father* stencil, 1970s
Collection of the artist

simply one layer and areas where there were maybe as many as nine layers. That all seemed to work together.

JS: Tell me more about the layers.

SK: I became more and more enamored with using transparent paints and building up color by putting either similar hues or varied or opposing hues over each other and making gradient tones. One of the things that I noticed right away is that the paint surface got richer and more complex, and I was able to repaint things many times. This is one thing that I found: that the color gets better and better the more you paint it. I only used translucent, transparent colors, and with acrylic, you can go over it.

JS: So it didn't feel like you were making two different paintings.

SK: The more complex it got, the more it seemed that I wanted to do both at the same time, so the vine images had a lot of detail that were very similar to the hair and beard; the curving hairs from the beard, head, and eyebrows began to mimic the patterning.

JS: Did you wonder if you might fail?

SK: I thought of it more as a challenge, and it wasn't clear to me how successfully I could handle it. I've seen a vision of unearthly splendor, and it was something that may have been most completely dealt with by a filmmaker, but that was never going to be me. I had to deal with it in terms of a still image. I realized I could do a painting that would be much more realistic from a distance than it would be as you got closer. I realized the color would begin to separate and contrast as you moved in on it. As I walked up to it, it began to challenge the coherence of the image; it became more and more prominent as I walked toward the painting. It was like being more and more stoned, I guess.

JS: As you get closer, it's like being more and more stoned?

SK: Yes. The colors separate from the black and white, the patterns separate from the image. That was an issue to deal with, and also an exciting thing for me. I was happy with it as I struggled with it.

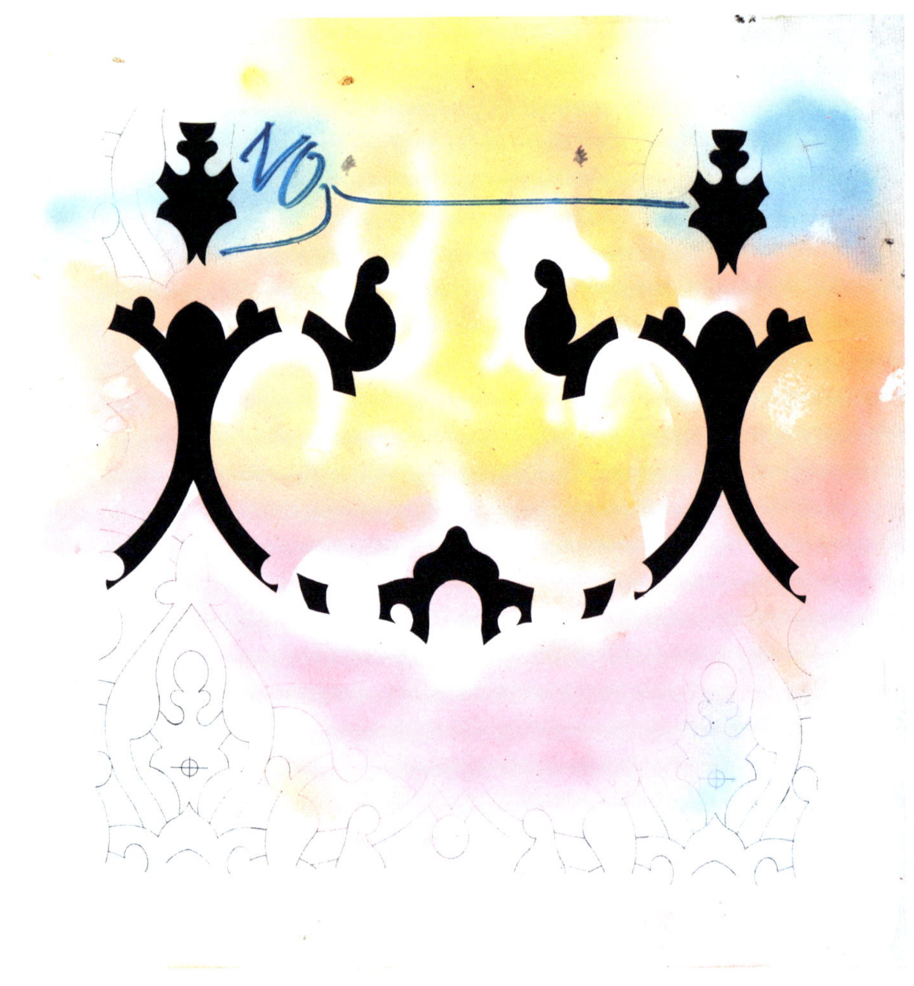

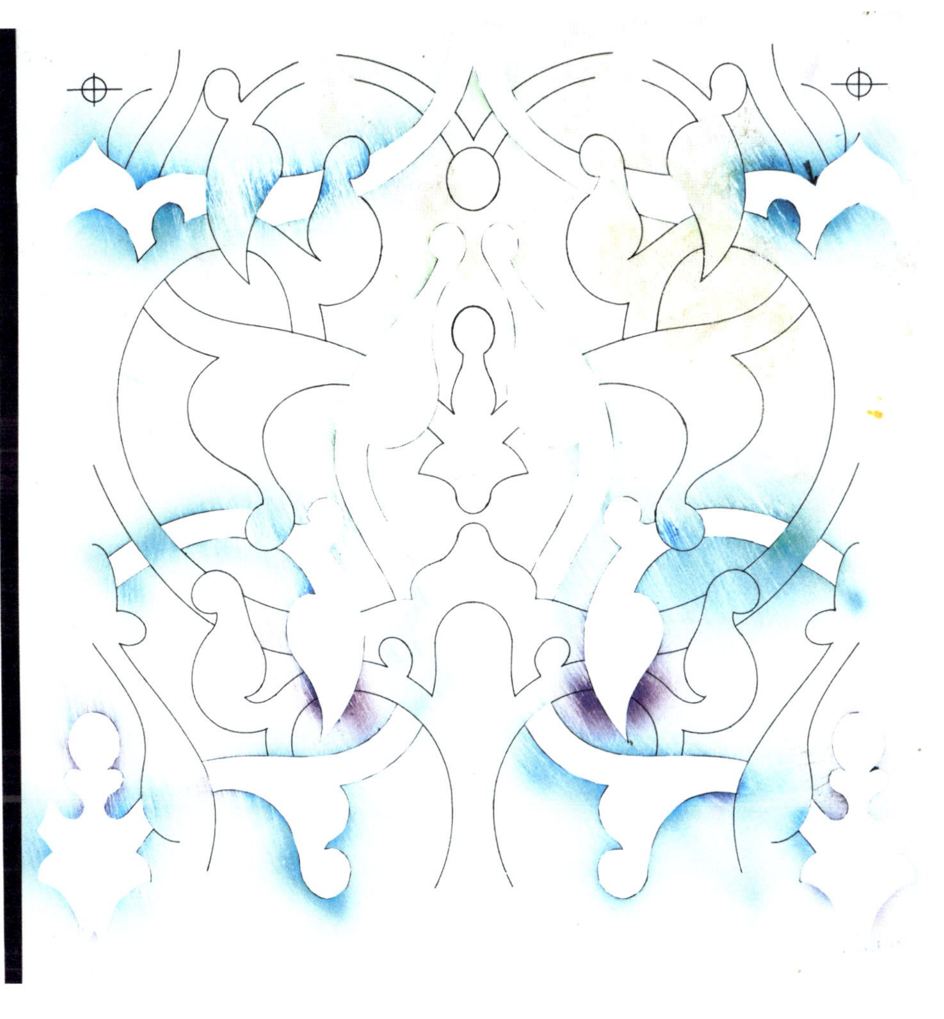

Stephen Kaltenbach, *Portrait of My Father* stencils, 1970s
Collection of the artist

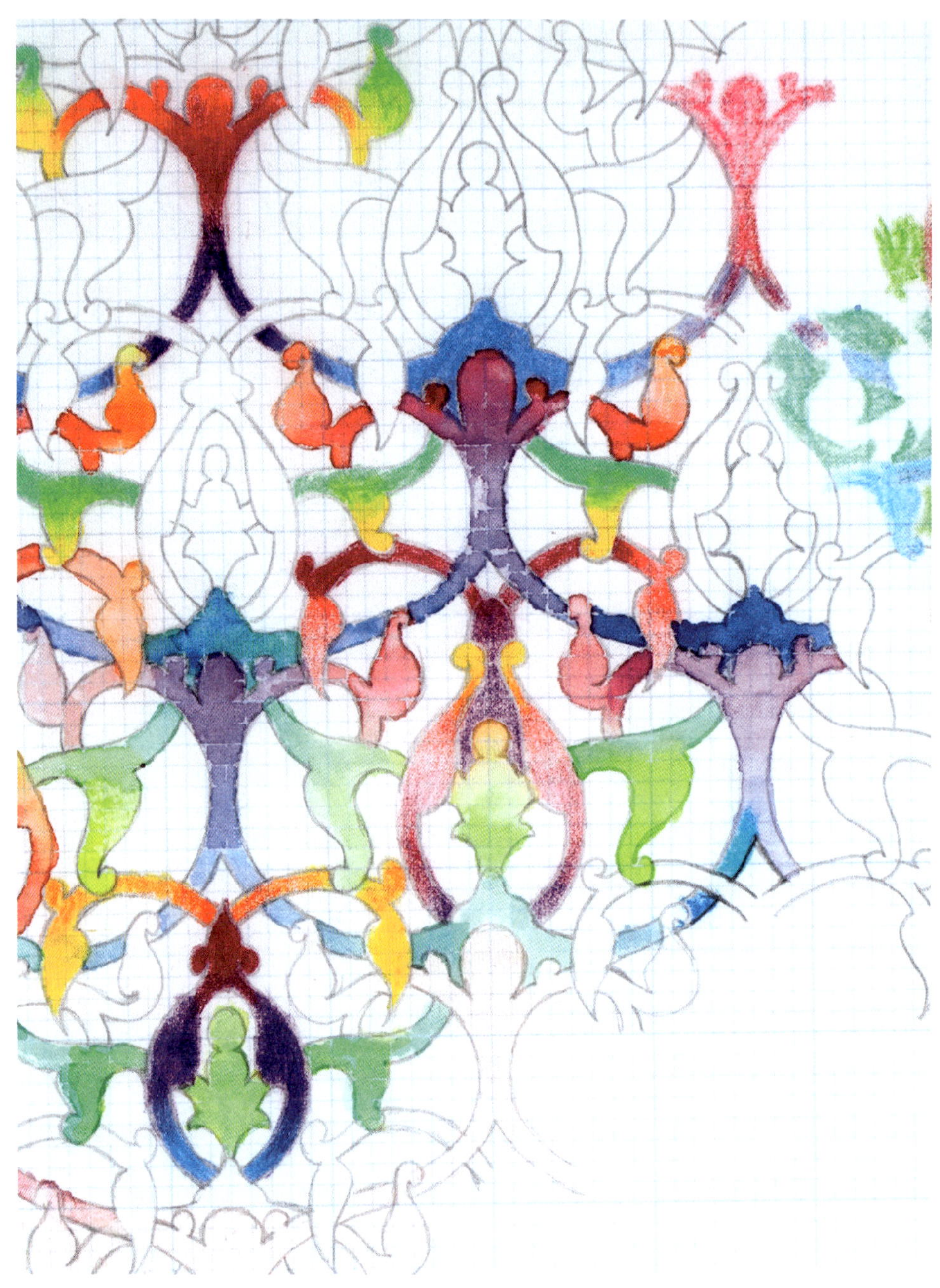

Stephen Kaltenbach, *Portrait of My Father* pattern study, 1970s
Collection of the artist

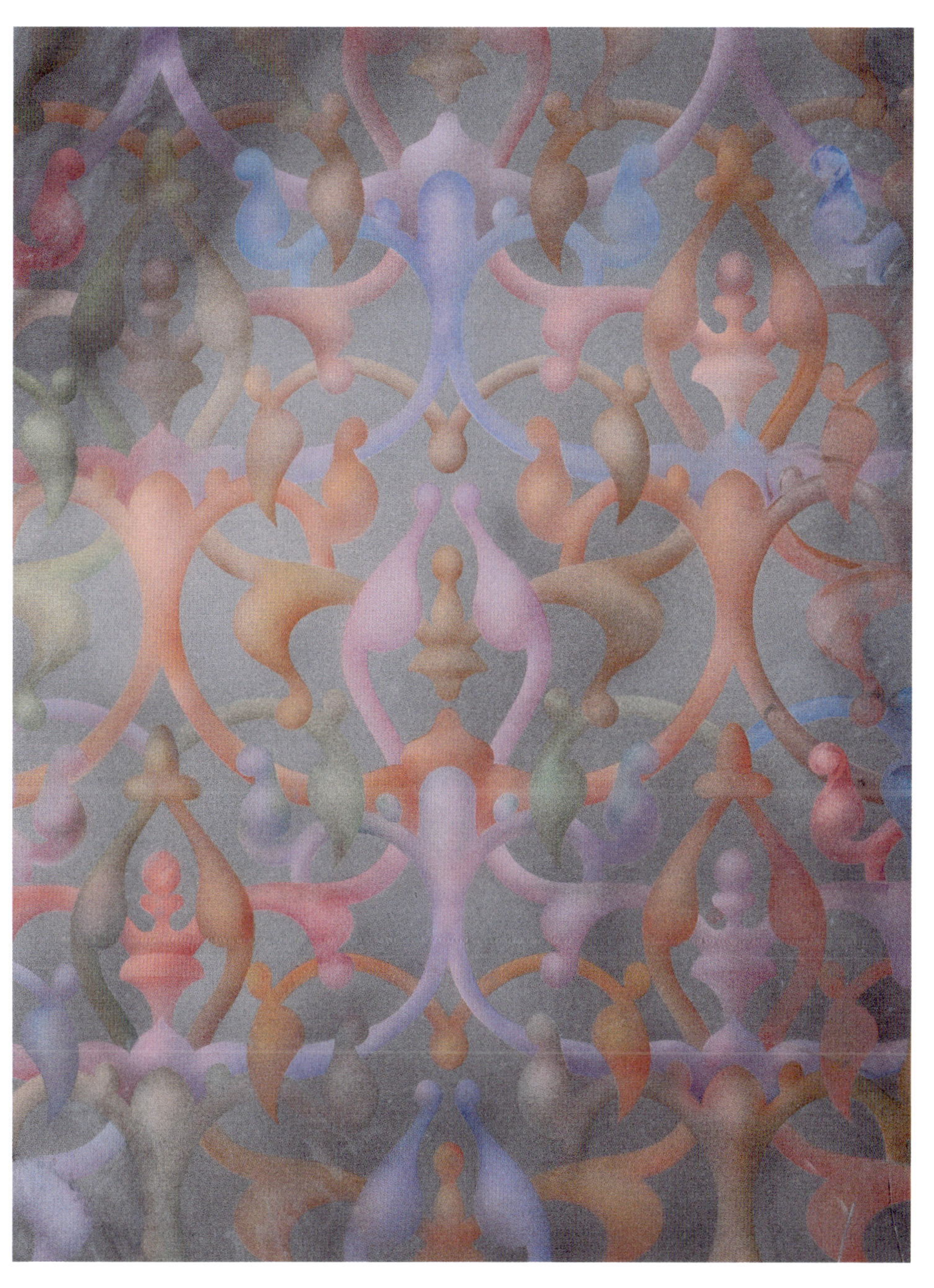

Portrait of My Father (dctail)

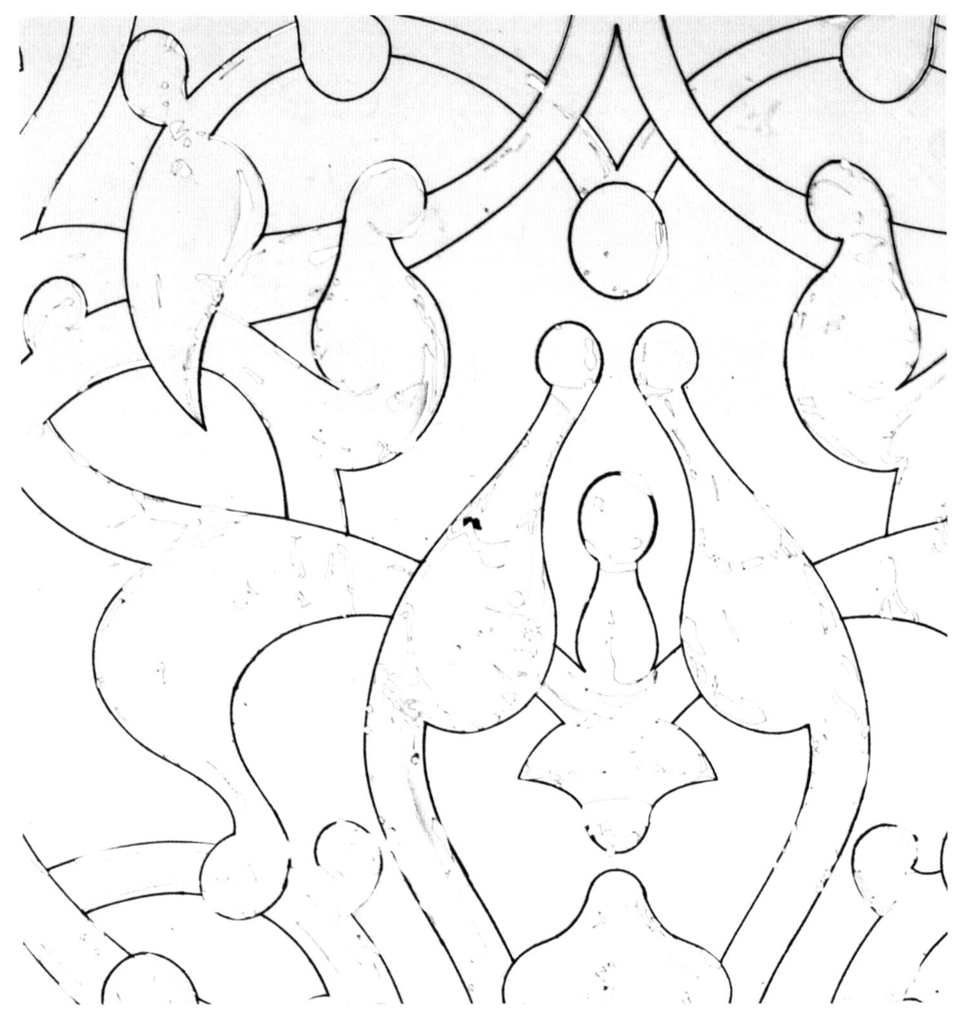

Stephen Kaltenbach, *Portrait of My Father* pattern study, 1970s
Collection of the artist

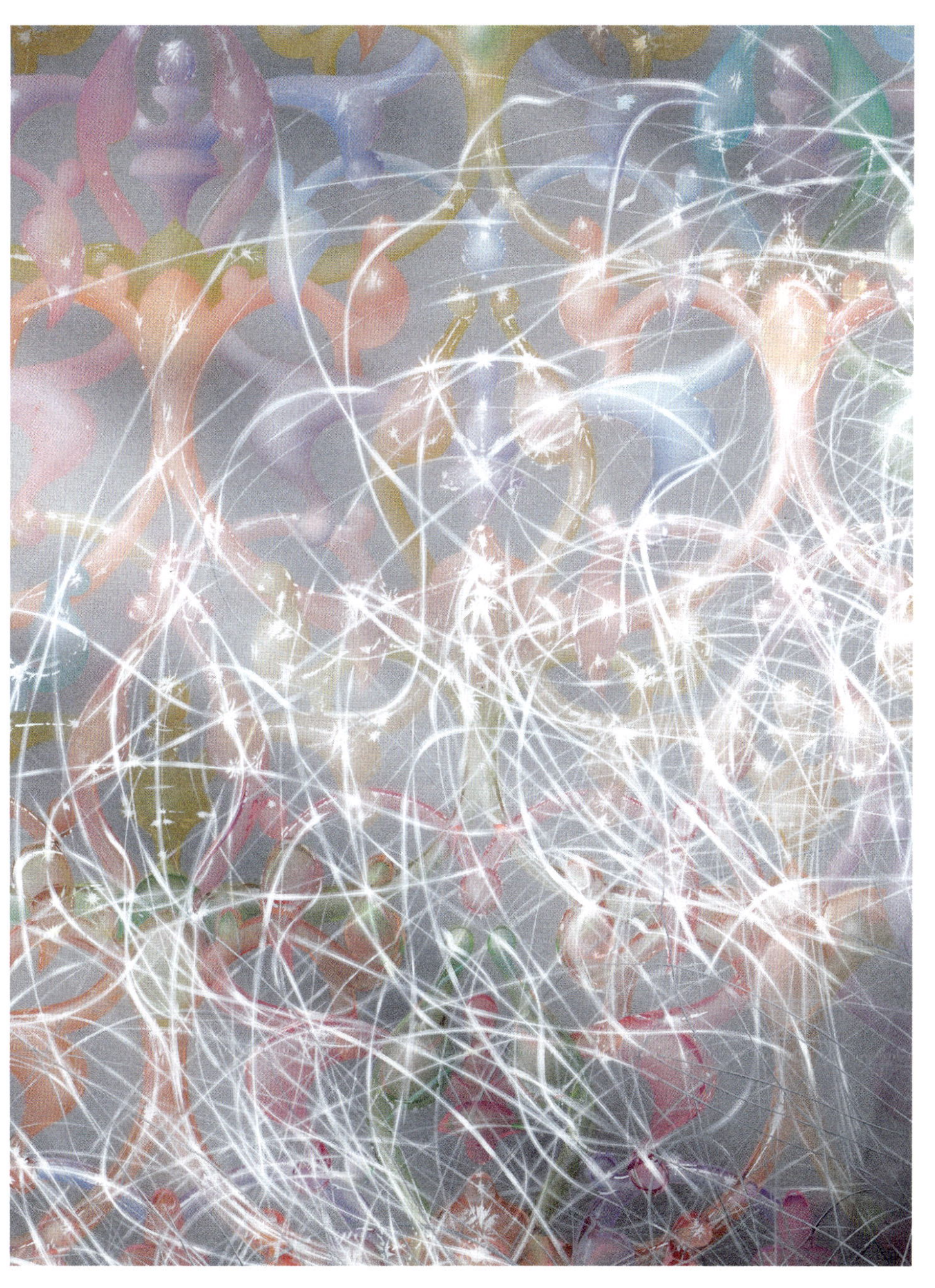

Portrait of My Father (detail)

JS: I know that drugs play an important part in your story. How did your relationship with drugs begin, and how are drugs connected to your work?

SK: I think that the pieces I'm most known for are the pieces that occurred to me when I was high.

I would have to say that drugs actually changed my mind. I think there is a way to trace my drug experience pretty much step by step to a worldview that I don't think I would hold now if I hadn't had those experiences. That's what drugs are for — to change your view of the world. It increased my vision and the kinds of things I was considering. Luckily, being an artist, you don't have to seem normal or usual, which I consider a tremendous advantage; I need to live my life as authentically as possible. I don't want to try to appear different than I am. I really don't.

> *We recorded these interviews by phone during a pandemic, but I regret not seeing his face at moments like these. Aren't you, Steve, a strange and shimmering example of someone who already appears quite different than they are? And many times over at that?*

I made it almost entirely through graduate school — within a few months of graduation — before I got high. I remember going over to my girlfriend's house, walking in the front door and seeing people lying all over the living room. Their eyes looked swollen and red, and they were kind of sweaty. Two of them decided they were going to get me stoned, which had a surprisingly strong effect on me.

In 1967, I was maybe a couple of weeks away from graduating, and the last meeting of the figure drawing class was happening: I was lucky to have been there stoned. The models were draping these long bolts of fabric around themselves, stretching it out, and making shapes with it. Suddenly the figures weren't necessary; the fabric was an amazing sculptural form, so flexible, so full of potential.

Mescaline is a nonsynthetic psychedelic that comes from the Mexican peyote and San Pedro cactus; its effects can last up to 13 hours and be quite intense. It was carried into the popular Western imagination by The Doors of Perception, *Aldous Huxley's 1954 trip chronicle. A memorable scene takes place at a local drug store, where the author encounters a stack of art books, including one on the early Renaissance painter Botticelli. The appearance of a dress in a work called* The Return of Judith to Bethulia *(ca. 1472) provokes a reflection on drapery as a major artistic theme, one affording profound abstract and lyrical passages in otherwise representational artworks.*

It's curious that abstraction would capture Huxley's attention rather than the head of Holofernes, which Judith's handmaiden carries in a small bowl resting on her head.

Kaltenbach experienced something similar high on weed, and later merged his fabric epiphanies with open-ended instructions. Reflecting on a sculpture made of felt called Modern Drapery *(1967), he subsequently wrote that it "left my studio with instructions that it was to be arranged and installed by the curator/gallerist/collector as they wished."*

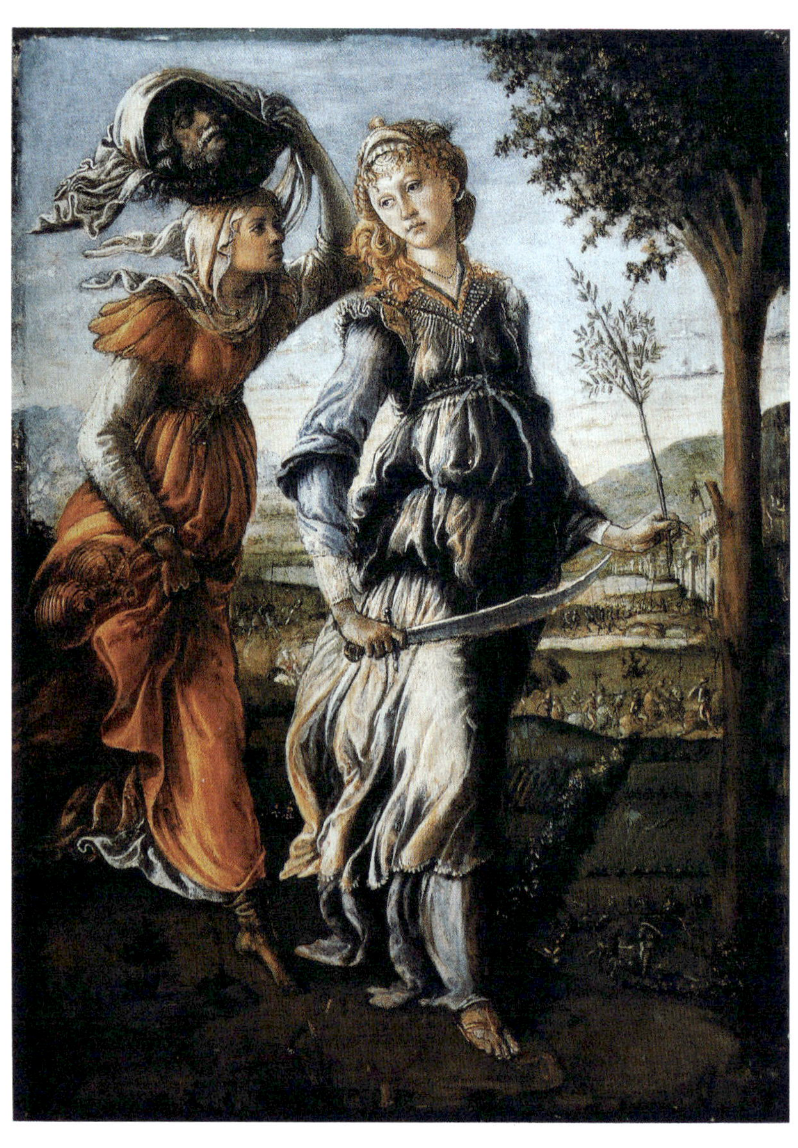

Sandro Botticelli, *The Return of Judith to Bethulia*, ca.1472
Oil on panel, 31 × 24 cm., Galleria degli Uffizi, Florence

Kaltenbach was most likely inspired by Morris, who, in a departure from the earlier, rigid, geometric dimensionality of his sculptures, began making felt works in the late 1960s that emphasize process, chance, and the indeterminacy of "soft" materials. Kaltenbach wanted others to complete his work.

I immediately left the class and got myself under control enough to make a drawing. I was awake all night, and my work evolved really fast. I decided that I needed to somehow unify the pedestal as part of the sculpture, but the first piece was very crude; I had a steel object strapped, sort of bolted to the pedestal. It got to the point where my sculptural work actually became part of the structure of the room.

Then I jumped from the unification of the sculpture and pedestal to the unification of the environment and sculpture. That was what I called "room alterations" or "room constructions." Within a week, I had a lot of drawings and a number of epiphanies. At first, they were simply engineering drawings, architectural drawings, and blueprints.

After my final review at Davis, a professor said, "It was lucky that you had these blueprints and drawings for the room alterations because we wouldn't have given you your degree without them."

I built my first room alteration or construction the summer after I graduated, in 1967, at [what was then] the San Francisco Museum of Art. I built a pyramid that filled the entire room. There was no flat floor in the room.

Kaltenbach's room constructions or alterations were conceived as a series of 24 drawings, later translated into precise blueprints. In addition to the work's debut at the San Francisco Museum of Art (later the San Francisco Museum of Modern Art, or SFMOMA), one was constructed in 1969 at the Whitney Museum of American Art under pioneering curator Marcia Tucker. The folded brochure included a series of questions written by the artist, including the following: "Is it important for an artist to be able to distinguish between manipulation of perception as a means for art expression from its manipulation as a result?"

By altering architectural space, Kaltenbach collapsed a distinction between container and contained, and — quite significantly for the time — turned the physicality of the gallery into the artwork. In his use of everyday materials like wood, drywall, and carpet, he also anticipated the anti-aesthetic strategies of postminimalism and, to a certain extent, institutional critique.

JS: Was taking psychedelics an ongoing part of your life in the barn?

SK: Maybe five times, maybe more, but not more than eight or nine times over the whole time I was living out there.

JS: So just once a year?

SK: Once a year or three times in a month and then nothing for three years. For me, that was a lot because I was very affected by

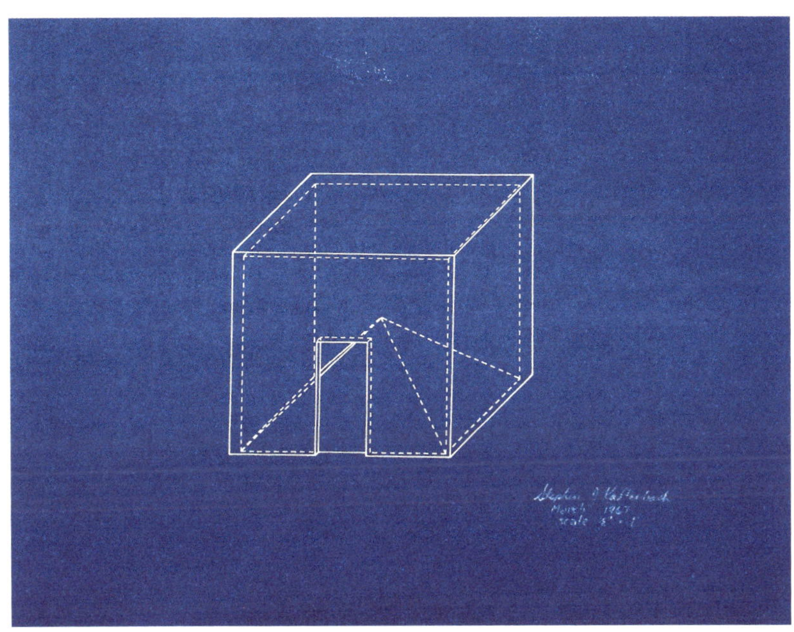

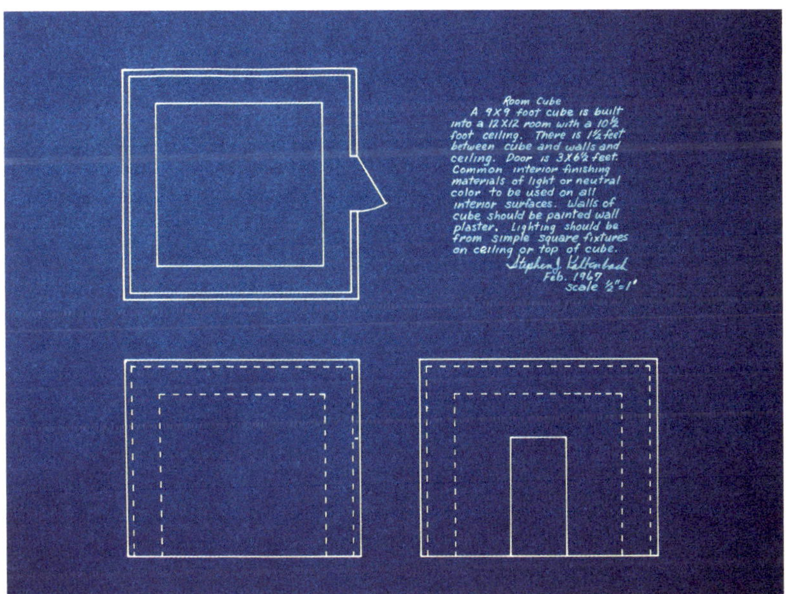

(top) Stephen Kaltenbach, *Peaked Floor (Room Construction)*, 1967, Blueprint; (bottom) Stephen Kaltenbach, *Room Cube (Isometric perspective)*, 1967, Blueprint, Courtesy the artist

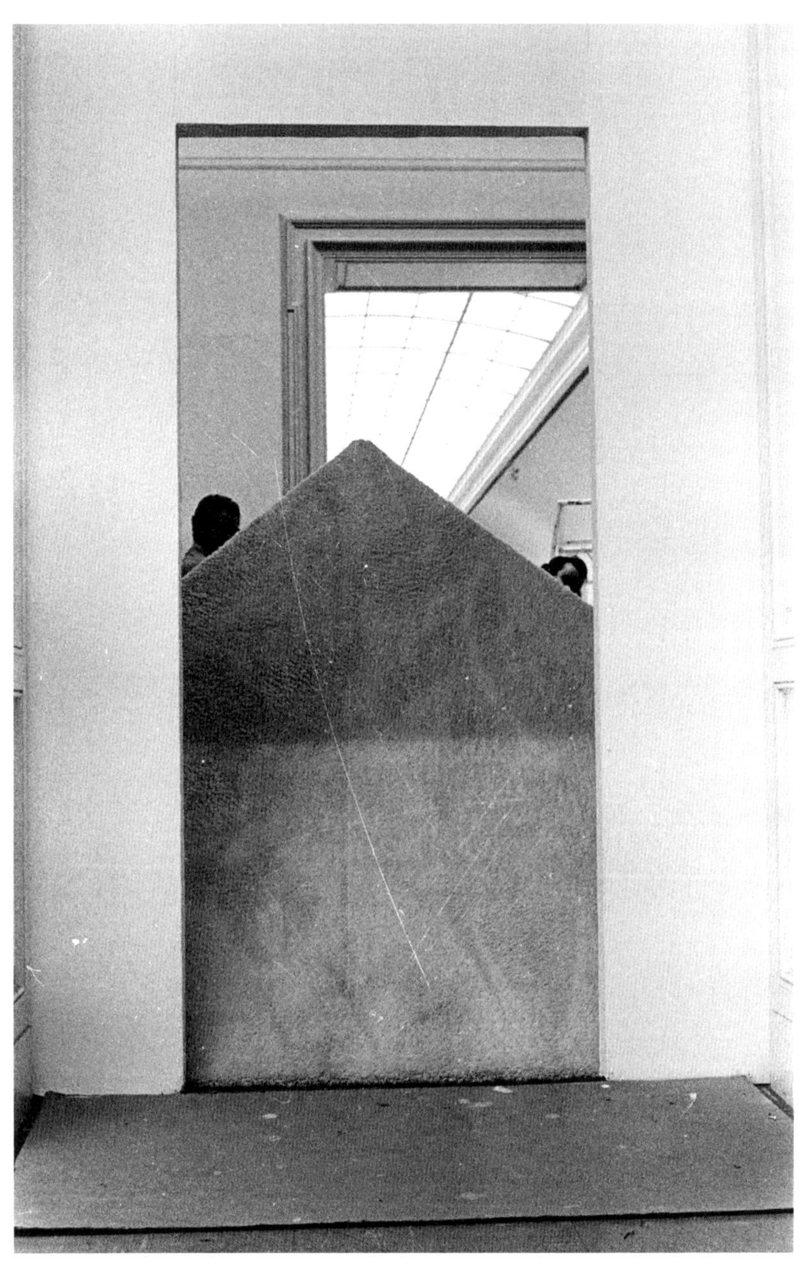

Stephen Kaltenbach with *Peaked Floor (Room Construction)*
at San Francisco Museum of Art, 1967, Photo: Gerald Walburg
Image courtesy San Francisco Museum of Modern Art

my psychedelic experiences. But I was still a conscientious person; I was able to teach my classes and drive to school and do all of the things I was supposed to do.

JS: I've read that you developed a relationship with God. How did that emerge, and what's the timeline of that related to the drugs?

SK: Things happen in my life that I see as momentous and life-guiding. While painting the portrait of my father, God the Father made himself known to me — unless I'm a schizophrenic, which certainly is a possibility in many people's minds. I went through a period of self-realization about my inner thoughts and feelings and hang-ups. I don't mean to freak you out or anything; maybe it's an experience that you need to have for yourself.

I was very close to my mom at the time, and we talked in detail about the whole thing. My poor mom had seven children, and all of them, except one, had psychedelic experiences and talked to her about it. Most of them were in Berkeley throughout the '60s and '70s.

Other people perceive their good fortune as luck, but I began to perceive God as taking care of me. God wants the best for me. I'm not naturally a good, kind, and moral person. If I veer away from his ideal, then I hear about it sometimes — sometimes pretty loudly. I can't even see the end of it, or I don't feel I have the consciousness to begin to investigate it. I'm suspicious of my own conclusions; I've done wrong before, yet I do think I am right about this. I can't come up with another explanation for my experiences other than that God is real, God speaks English, knows the future, and has a plan for me; he cares about how I live my life.

JS: Far out.

SK: One time, after I had already established a connection with God, we were talking about this thing I was worried about. I wasn't freaking out, but I was very open about saying, "I believe I could die if I do what I think you want me to do, so that concerns me. I do know that you want the best for me, so I just need to know what to do."

This brings us into something that's uncomfortably close to people who knock on your door on Saturday mornings. You see people standing there holding a Bible. I'm not trying to change your mind, OK, Jordan? [laughs]

JS: I don't sense that.

SK: OK, good. I'll give you one example that's pretty off the wall: I saw an angel. I was not stoned. It looked like a 12-year-old boy, just radiating a tremendous amount of light. No wings and sitting on a marble wall that was quite luminescent and very, very beautiful. He slowly turned and held my gaze for a moment, smiled a little bit, and slowly disappeared.

JS: And you were completely sober?

SK: Completely sober, and I remain so. If there's something to celebrate, an opening or something, I sometimes have a martini. I'm not a teetotaler or anything, but I really dislike being at all high.

I'm not saying there's no chemical basis for what I have to say, which I realize is sometimes part of religious experiences. I have come out to my studio, usually in the middle of the night when I'm not sleeping, and I'm just here in a kind of meditative state, and very often I'm in conversation with God. Sorry, I sound like a nut, I know.

JS: No sorrys here.

SK: It seemed to me that there were spirits that were somehow restricted from appearing in the world, but if you took psychedelics you could experience them. If there is a God, I don't even know how to think about it. If it's someone who is interested in me, especially if it's someone who actually loves me, then he should be able to prove himself to me. That should be easy. I thought about it for quite a while and I decided, *OK, this is going to be my LSD trip. I'm going to get high and I'm going to address God*: "I don't mean to be impertinent or anything like that, but I don't know whether you're real or not. It's seeming likely that you might be, and so I'm just asking you, if you are real, if you would please let me know."

I got my, I think it was blotter acid on a little piece, tiny square of paper, and I had it in my hand. I was going to take it with a glass of water, and I realized the radio was on. I listened to public radio, classical music. I decided to turn it off, and I believe I was walking over toward it when the music stopped and this voice came on. It's this guy who introduced himself as a tantric teacher. He said, "I want to introduce my remarks by telling you the difference between tantric practice and yoga."

He said, "In yoga, they meditate for 5,000 lifetimes until they become clear enough to realize there is absolutely nothing they can do to make themselves worthy of God, then they surrender to God. In tantric, we surrender right now." When I heard that, I felt like, "OK, I've just been given my process, or my approach, or my attitude, that I can go into my conversation with, that I need to tell God if he will show me that there's someone out there to surrender to, I will do it."

JS: Sorry, this is after you take the blotter?

SK: I hadn't taken it yet. I was standing there with it in my hand. It was almost like I got the marching orders. This is something that's continued to this day in my life; when I get information like this, it's always either when I'm asking for it or somehow at the appropriate time. Usually, the more I need it, the stronger it is. Anyway, it was really clear to me that this was a pretty big coincidence and I thought I could trust it. I took it, got high, and sat down to address God. I said that if he would make himself known to me, I would obey and work for him and do his will for the rest of my life to my utmost ability. It's a promise that's pretty hard to live up to and I have had some failures, but it's been my general method since then.

JS: Got it. You were absolutely ready to surrender.

SK: I immediately heard words in English, and I remember them very, very clearly, it's very easy to remember. The words were, "We're going to clean up your act." At that point, my life kind of fell apart. I had a relationship that was not — I don't want to go into detail, but it wasn't very ethical, and it definitely was something I needed to be out of, and it fell apart immediately, within a few days.

I went through a self-reassessment that was very valuable, but not comfortable. I would say, "Just let me know what to do and I'll do it." People became rather worried about me because, well, you probably realize by now that I'm a person who doesn't keep secrets. If they're not art, I don't keep them real well. Especially if you're teaching art, I venture that you have to let yourself show. I was very open about the fact that God was speaking to me and that God spoke English. My friends and my peers at Sac State began to both avoid and be very worried about me.

When I took drugs, I learned that a relationship with God is a personal thing that people have within their power to establish and develop. What Christians would call "witnessing," when you tell of your experience with God, with me a lot of it is pretty undependable because of my history with drugs. LSD is almost like a kind of artificial temporary psychosis. I know what the experience is and yet I don't, weirdly enough, feel very qualified to talk about it.

When I began to work on the painting of Dad, I began to consider these experiences as divine. It seemed like there was tremendous serendipity beginning to take shape in my life where things were just falling into place.

I began to see the pattern as representative of a portrait of God the Father, and the image of the man as representative of my earthly father. And I primarily wanted the upper-right-hand corner to be open to represent my father facing God at the end of his existence.

I talked to other people about it, and they would say things like, "You can't prove God is real. If he is real, he is on a different plane, a different dimension. It's categorically beyond research." I thought, "Well, OK. That seems actually like it's probably right."

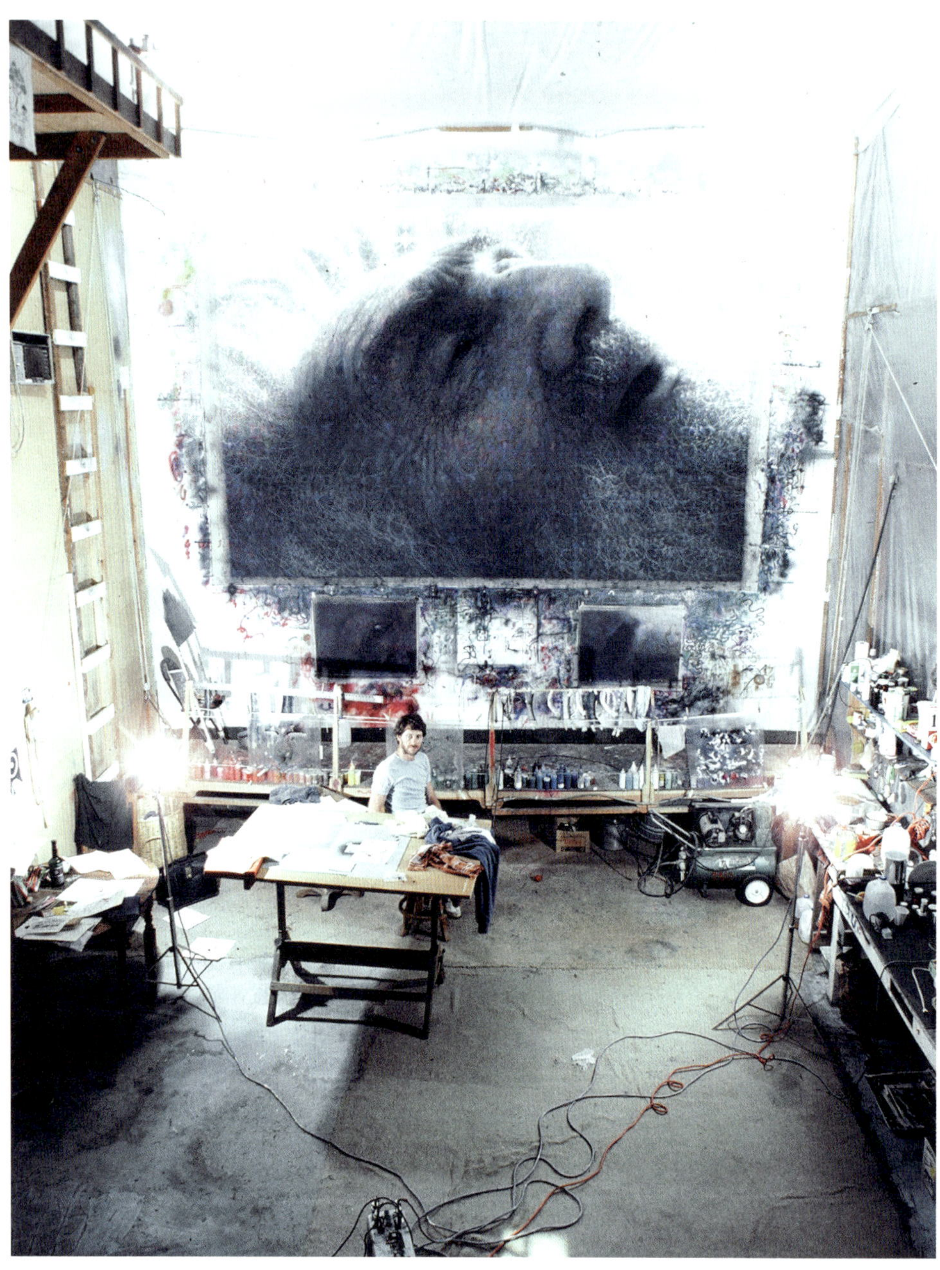

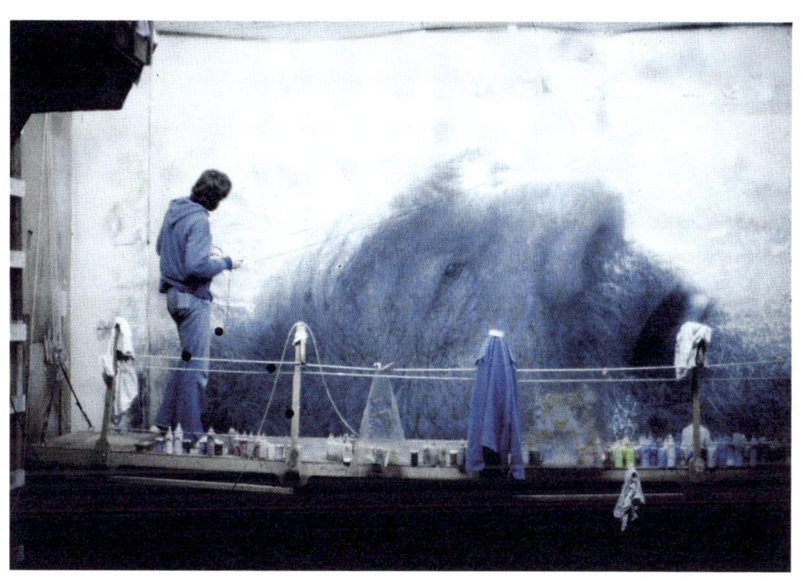

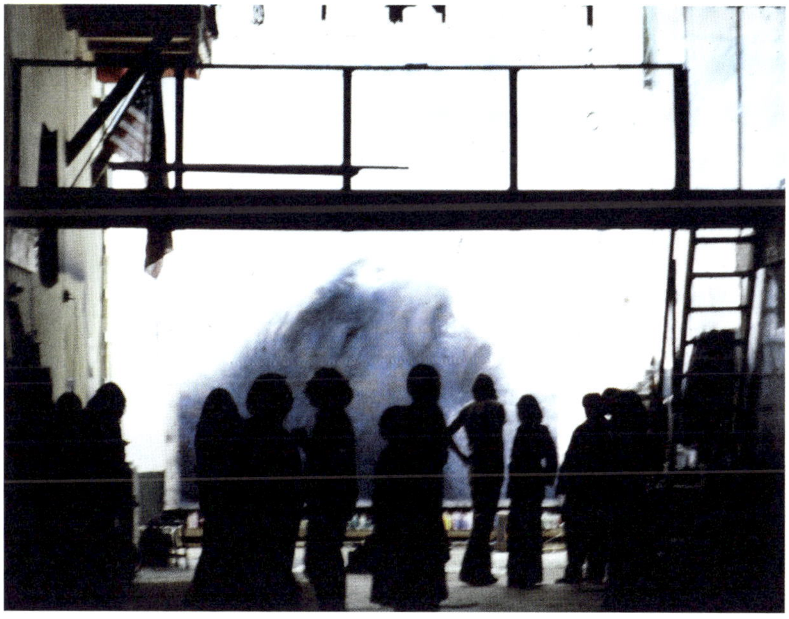

Stephen Kaltenbach, *Portrait of My Father* in progress, 1970s
Photographer unknown, Images courtesy the artist

ABSTRACTION AND REPRESENTATION

Art historical categories tend to be inherited and binary. Perhaps the most timeworn is the distinction between what we understand as abstraction and representation. Traditionally, these categories are as separate as portrait and landscape, vertical and horizontal. One might say that Portrait of My Father *is representative in its rendering of a person (what Kaltenbach refers to as an "image") and abstract in its patterning, which does not correspond to objects in real space and time. One might also say that the work is dedicated not just to the possibilities of representation, but also to its limits —*
in its excess of information, Portrait *takes the viewer beyond fact, suggesting the unknowability of self, time, and history. In its insistence on both pattern and image, the painting establishes an equivalence between beard hairs and the mystical doings of the universe. It further unites (and also detonates) commonly held categorical distinctions such as secular and religious, terrestrial and otherworldly, specific and immeasurable.*

SK: By late 1978 my worldview had changed to the point where I was living in a way that was obviously not normal at all. School was off for five weeks for winter break. I would pray, ask God what he planned for me that day, and do what I felt I should do. It wasn't like I would speak to him and get my marching orders for the day or anything like that. It was very intuitive, and it was a time of low efficiency that I was feeling this new relationship. I didn't really know that much about him, so I didn't have that much to say about the situation. Slowly, maybe unfortunately, I had more and more to say about it as my experiences multiplied.

JS: How did you talk to God?

SK: This is even more questionable, so I'm delighted to tell you about it. I had been occasionally consulting the I Ching. After God spoke to me, I thought, "I'm going to cast the coins in him." I asked God a question and cast the coins. I don't know if you have any experience with the I Ching.

JS: It's been a while.

SK: I think that's an amazing book. For me, it's always seemed to be applicable, unless I was being impertinent. Is that even the word?

JS: Sure.

SK: Impertinent. Pushing it too far and being demanding about information. It always seemed to answer me on topic. I said, "I heard that you know the future. Is that true?" The answer was positive, and within a very short time, I think I asked him two or three questions.

One time, I actually heard this pretty extensive instruction from God saying, "Put away the book and put away two of the coins. Just use one coin and ask me questions that I can answer with either yes or no." I did that and talked to him for an hour or two. I never got the wrong answer in a couple of hours. I continued to do that when I needed to. It wasn't common, but I would use a coin and I'd ask, "Should I do this or not?"

His responses have taken many different forms over the years. I found one of my books where I've kept a record of the things I've sought God's response to, and it's full.

JS: Did you start going to church?

SK: I heard from God that I needed to become a Christian and begin to go to church. I actually had the temerity to enter an argument with God. I said, "Look, I have a personal relationship with you where we can talk together; you have proven your reality to me by constantly overwhelming the odds. Things aren't like a single coincidence, but a triple coincidence, and it just happens all the time."

From the outside, people can say, "You're involved in magical thinking." My observation is that it's something quite real.

"As I understand it, you're asking me to trade that for a dogmatic relationship with history, with the Bible, with the opinions of Bible teachers," and so on. "I don't want to trade personal experience for, at best, what would be a scholarly relationship with what happened." Not that that stuff is not interesting to me, but that's what I was afraid of.

What I got back from God was, "You are going to become even closer to me, and it's going to remain personal." It was an absolute promise that it wasn't going to become dogmatic, and it hasn't.

JS: Wow. And you were experiencing bad stuff, too, no? Tell me more about the more negative psychological disturbances you were experiencing.

SK: Well, as good as that mescaline trip was, I had an acid trip that was equally bad. This was right around the time when I was finishing the painting, getting ready to leave the barn. I'm not going to make claims for the reality of the experience I had, but I felt a spiritual visitation from low-life spiritual beings. Oh, my goodness. Well, let's accept that I had taken LSD, so let's just say that could have been a pure hallucination. A horrible being was there with me in the barn and was really disgusting. It was talking about people killing me. Within a couple days, I got a warning that someone was making threatening remarks about me.

I was also dealing with this kind of shaken reality where my worldview was being pushed toward accepting — I mean, I was a Zen Buddhist, and I was being pushed toward considering a new spiritual reality.

JS: Somewhere in my notes, although I'm not sure now where I got it, there's mention of a 20-hit experience. Is that true?

SK: How did that information survive?

JS: I don't actually remember. Is that a real thing?

SK: Yes and no. [both laugh]

JS: Explain.

SK: It seems like that may be hard to achieve, but here's what happened.

It was at that period when I thought, "It's possible that I'm just not getting high enough to get beyond this lowdown, bad stuff." I had purchased a lot of … what's the Indian or Chinese root that people take for …

JS: Ginger?

SK: No …

JS: Turmeric?

SK: No, not turmeric. It's much more powerful. Rats. I would love to get the name of it in this recording. It looks like the lower part from the waist down of a human figure. Sometimes, there's two roots together and people take it for medicinal purposes …

Anyway, I had a lot of it. I took the LSD and I heard God say, "I want you to grind up all of this root and take it right now." That was immediately after I took this acid. I did that. I put it in a blender, mixed it with water until it was a sticky, frothy liquid. It tasted like tree bark or something, and I drank it. And I didn't experience anything.

JS: Ginseng?

SK: Ginseng! There it is. [both laugh]

JS: You took 20 hits of acid and then you received instructions to consume all of your ginseng?

SK: Yes, I can't explain. [laughs] I know, it's weird. It's too late to appear normal. Let's just have the information available and let people do what they want to do with it.

When you called this morning, I was walking my dog, and I hadn't quite gotten back to the house. I wear a mask when I go out, and I was thinking, "I can't wear a mask when I'm doing this interview," because as you probably know, "hypocrite" comes from the Greek, to wear a mask. To me, that is the worst of all sins. Partially, it's so bad because it's so bound to be unsuccessful. People are going to find you out no matter what, and hurray for that.

JS: Let it out!

SK: [laughs] What was the question again?

JS: [laughs] 20 hits of acid, ginseng.

SK: Right. I took it. I thought, *This is dangerous, but I'm feeling crazy right now, and I really want to make contact.* I can't remember if it was before or after my contact with God. I don't believe I used the coin to ask yes or no. I'm not certain it was English. I just suddenly knew I needed to take all that ginseng, and so I did. I fully expected to get really high.

    I think Lozano, when she took LSD every day for a month, I don't think she was ever the same after that, mentally. It wasn't a good thing for her. As I've stated, I did not notice any difference in my mentality.

JS: To confirm, you were completely sober, even though you'd taken 20 hits?

SK: Yes, I didn't count them, but it was all that I had. I'd had it for quite a while. I don't know, maybe it got weaker or something. That would be something to research. I do wonder if they know if ginseng counteracts psychedelic drug exposure or anything like that.

JS: Thanks for clearing that up.

SK: I'm a little surprised that that's available in the information out there on me. [laughs] I do tend to say more than I should.

On several occasions in the past decade, Kaltenbach has amplified his choice to leave New York by explaining that his departure, and everything since — including Portrait — *has been one big piece, a gesamtkunstwerk too big and complex to entirely wrap one's arms around. In at least three interviews, he has defined the terms of his move as one of intentionally seeking "regional artist" status, a choice in keeping with his "Protocol."*

He has also framed his actions within something he calls both his "Elephant Project" and "Black Project." Black, presumably, because of his work in the shadows, and elephant on account of its size.

In our conversations, I didn't ask about these overarching projects. I felt (and feel) that the existence of Portrait of My Father *was real enough to render such concerns temporarily beside the point, especially if he didn't offer them up. But I'm surprised he didn't. He certainly knows that an artwork is an artwork if he says it is, even if it's reverse engineered, intended to perplex, or invented as a bid for credit.*

Here's how he put it in the hipster magazine Vice, *of all places, on the occasion of a small, 2016 exhibition in New York:*

"I felt strongly that my work needed time to mature in private to gain the gravitas necessary to operate as I wanted it to [...] I would leave the contemporary art world and re-establish myself as a regional artist, maybe a painter or a sculptor. Meanwhile I could continue my conceptual work in private without the constant

examination that went with New York's exposure. I, of course, had my own ambitions so this was difficult but I was very interested in forcing myself to do 'hard things.' I referred to this work as the Elephant Project *or sometimes the* Black Project*."*

And in Roger White's 2015 essay, "The End": "Kaltenbach has said that it will continue until he has a retrospective at a museum, at which point the game will be up [...] 'I realized I could do this really big project,' he said. 'I decided I wanted to create a regional artist. I wanted to make him as good as possible, but have his concerns be OFF enough that it wouldn't really be received by the avant-garde world. [...] [a]nd that has worked for a long time. But I think in many ways it's beginning to fail. Because some of the work I've done is now being taken seriously.'"

It is and it isn't. Kaltenbach's retrospective exhibition — and his first solo museum presentation in the United States in nearly 40 years — opened on January 26, 2020, at the Manetti Shrem Museum of Art at the University of California, Davis. The Beginning and The End, *curated by Constance Lewallen and Ted Mann, was slated to run through May 10, but closed just six weeks later because of the statewide Covid-19 lockdowns. For an artist invested in withholding, it was both a cruel and amusing irony.*

Of the Elephant/Black Project, *Sarah Lehrer-Graiwer writes, "[t]he work is so utterly convincing and faithfully carried out — like flawless Method acting or a one-to-one scale model — that it is basically imperceptible as art and suggests that being 'of art' may be beside the point. The project acutely risks nonrecognition, defying our expectations of what is necessary to make a piece perceptible as a piece."* She also notes that *"Kaltenbach showed a genius for wrong choices and comically perverse moves."*

Lehrer-Graiwer's perspective is likely informed by her Lozano scholarship, which includes 2014's Dropout Piece, *a book-length study of a potentially nonexistent artwork. "Lee Lozano's legendary and legendarily elusive* Dropout Piece, *begun around 1970, may or may not be precisely equivalent to her dropping out of the New York art world,"* *it begins. "It is among Lozano's most challenging works and notorious, lasting achievements. Yet in many ways there is no piece to speak of, not in any conventional sense of an artwork we can exhibit and study, nor of a performance that took place as an event for an audience."* Indeed, *"*Dropout Piece *takes material form only in a few notes the artist wrote to herself in a private notebook on 5 April 1970 — not in an art object, drawing, document or discretely prepared entity of any kind."* Once Lozano split New York, she either never made artwork again or did nothing but.

JS: How about non-drug-related setbacks?

SK: I suffered these periods of having to stop working because I didn't know what to do next. Eventually, I think in the last two years, I fell into this rhythm that I really liked. When I was working, I would go back and sit down and look at the painting and I'd find the area that I liked the least and I would decide what I wanted to do with it. Then I would use a piece of drafting tape and tiny little notes, like, "Paint more hairs, make them darker."

I would say that a lot of the time out there I was really very happy and in a state that required all my attention. If your attention is completely committed, then you have really nothing left over for normal neurotic grinding about. There's no, "Oh, poor me."

I had a viewing platform that was about nine feet up off the floor with a stairway going up to where I could sit at the back, or friends who came to visit could sit and view the painting. The bottom of the canvas was five or six feet from the floor. I had this excess of wall space, it was 18 feet tall, after all, and the light seemed to come in better from higher up. I thought that it would be easier to deal with the cold than the heat. I didn't like the heat very much and painted wearing only my Speedo. There were some superhot summers, and it was a steel building, so when it was 105 outside, it was at least that inside. I'd be drenched with sweat and wearing my Speedo. I could have been wearing nothing; I had total privacy. I always had the door locked.

From the platform, I would make a plan. I'd execute those changes and then I'd go back and see what I did. Virtually every time, I would make further changes to that area until I would see another area that I thought was working less well, and so I would shift and work on that area.

At some point I made a very punk decision to make one side predominantly green and the other side predominantly red. I don't know why. Once I got the idea, I couldn't resist it. I thought I could do it and it wouldn't show. And people don't generally talk about it, so maybe I was right. It may have been a stupid idea.

While it's subtle in the swirl of the picture plane, a viewer may indeed sort the green from the red side. It's most visible in the bottom corners.

JS: Is there anything else that you think we should address about the actual painting?

SK: Oh, OK, the stuff that you might not have seen?

JS: Yes.

SK: There are no eyelashes.

JS: There are no eyelashes.

SK: I tried to put them in, and I didn't like it. I liked it better without them.

JS: So you painted them out?

SK: I painted them on when it was cold and humid, so the acrylic wouldn't dry right away. I was using a retarder. I rushed down, got back, and thought, *Oh, that's not good,* and so I used a wet cloth and wiped them off and tried it again, then wiped them off again. I think after, like, the third time, I decided, *Oh, you do kind of like it the way it is.*

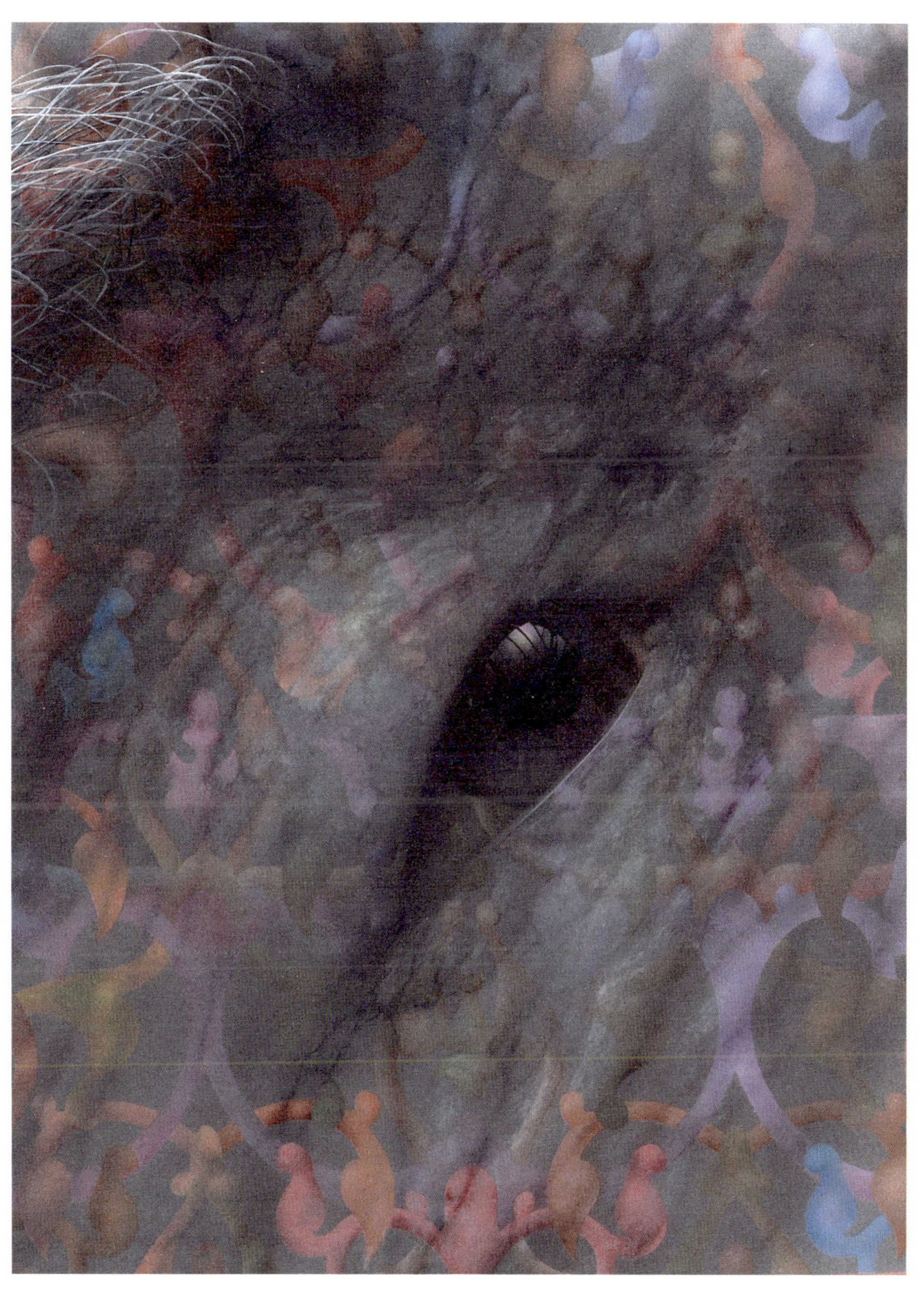

Portrait of My Father (detail)

SK: If you tell somebody you're seeing things that aren't there, they're going to worry about your mental state. My friend John Fitz Gibbon was just a little bit out there, too, so we were able to get along really pretty well.

He was very concerned about my well-being. Toward the end of the project he was coming out to visit me almost every day. One time he showed up and said, "Look, you're probably going to paint this thing to death. I'm concerned about you. I've arranged for a show at the Crocker Museum, and I want you to consider doing it and calling the painting finished." I agreed.

> *John Fitz Gibbon (1934-2009) was an art history professor at Sacramento State for two decades and recruited a number of artists to teach in the department, including Kaltenbach. He was also a prolific art critic, collector of postwar Californian art, and host of an art criticism-themed KPFA radio show. He wrote on many local artists, including Robert Arneson, Elmer Bischoff, Joan Brown, Robert Colescott, Richard Diebenkorn, and Jim Nutt.*
>
> *In a 1971* Art in America *piece titled "Sacramento!," he noted that "fear for one's reputation is at a world-minimum in Northern California."*
>
> *Fitz Gibbon wrote a detailed and rather over-the-top essay about* Portrait of My Father *in the 16-page brochure accompanying the Crocker exhibition: "His* Portrait of My Father *deserves to be recognized as the most elevated account of psychedelic experience in art and as one of the most concrete records of religious exaltation available to us in the art of our century. [...]*

In a work which so invokes the unconscious operations of Mind, the curvaceous, interlocking yab-yum of the repeating motif provides a sensual undercurrent of continuous sexual hum which great works of art, even when they are more about Death rather than about Love or Birth, are seldom wholly without."

He also contradicts the artist's hailstorm story regarding the origins of the painting Sunset, writing that it was "painted over a period of months from a photograph taken outside his studio, looking westward toward the Berryessa range."

When I checked in with Kaltenbach about this discrepancy, he said that Fitz Gibbon was almost always right, but in this case was wrong, adding that somewhere he had a photographic slide of the dents made by the three-inch hailstones. At the time of this publication, such slides have not been found.

SK: I did feel that maybe it would be a good idea to look into moving out. Toward the end of my stay at the barn, I bought a house trailer and parked it out out back. It was a little bit nicer, and it did have a bathroom.

JS: Were you as candid about your relationship with God as you were about your relationship with drugs when the painting debuted?

SK: I was just starting to talk about it. I was only 39 when I showed the painting at the Crocker. The opening reception was an absolute mob scene because I was upfront about my use of psychedelics informing the painting. I said that the painting was based on the inspiration that I received from my mescaline trip. There were

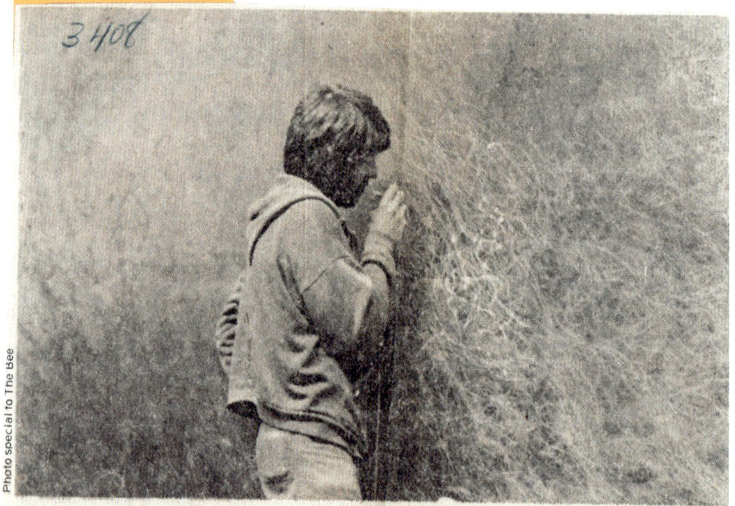

Steven Kaltenbach will continue to work on "Portrait of My Father" while the monumental painting is on view at the E.B. Crocker Gallery through March 11.

The work, with a section of the beard shown here, measures 10 by 15 feet.

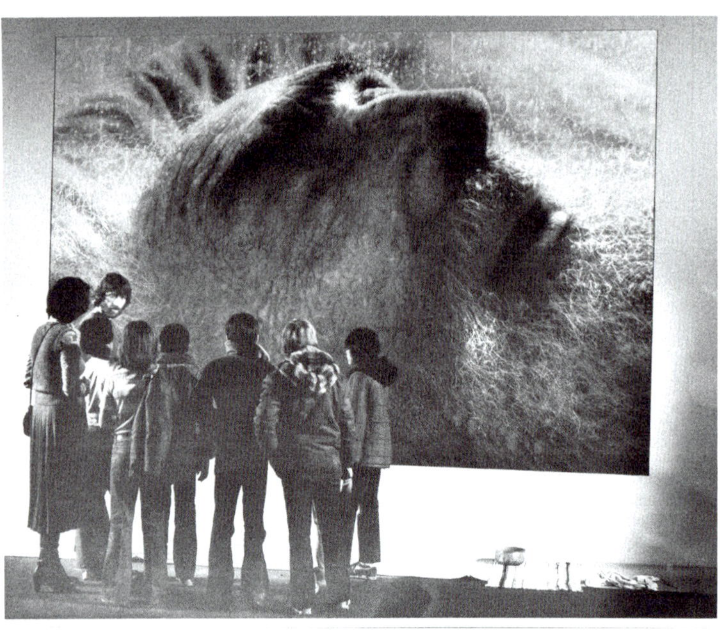

(top) *The Sacramento Bee*, date unknown, 1979 (bottom) The artist surrounded by children and painting supplies, Crocker Art Museum, 1979, Courtesy Crocker Art Museum

a huge number of people at my opening, and TV crews. I think they were curious about the drug connection.

The painting was installed opposite the elevator. From that distance, about 100 feet, the pattern pretty much goes away, and it becomes a very realistic image.

JS: I'm holding the original catalogue here — a modest, stapled thing — and the title of the original 1979 show is noteworthy: *Portrait of My Father*, all in caps, and then in little lowercase letters, *a painting in progress*.

> *I didn't realize until the tail end of editing this book that his name was misspelled throughout as "Steven," even on the front cover.*
>
> *The catalog includes Fitz Gibbon's essay, black and white reproductions, and a checklist of all 22 works on view — not just* Sunset, Stoned Maple, *and* Portrait, *but also studies in the form of photographs, drawings, and paintings.*

JS: The first time the painting is shown, you and the museum made explicit that it's, well, that it's not done. Was presenting the work more about process to you than the finished work?

SK: I made a deal with John and the curator, Roger Clisby, a very nice guy, that I would continue to work on the painting when it was displayed at the Crocker. I was going back in and tinting the black and white paint. We're talking a couple of square millimeters or centimeters. I was doing little tiny things with these small brushes.

JS: Was this after hours or during the day?

STEVEN KALTENBACH: **PORTRAIT OF MY FATHER**

a painting in progress

E. B. Crocker Art Gallery
Sacramento 1979

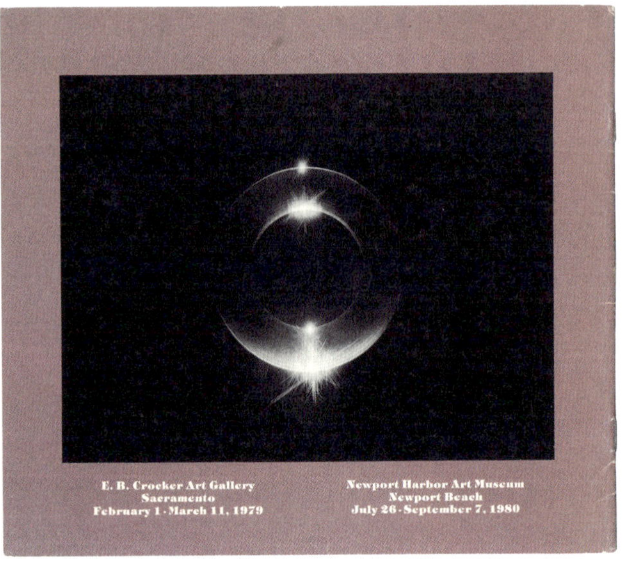

Steven Kaltenbach: Portrait of My Father: A Painting in Progress
(title page and back cover) E.B. Crocker Art Gallery, Sacramento, 1979

164

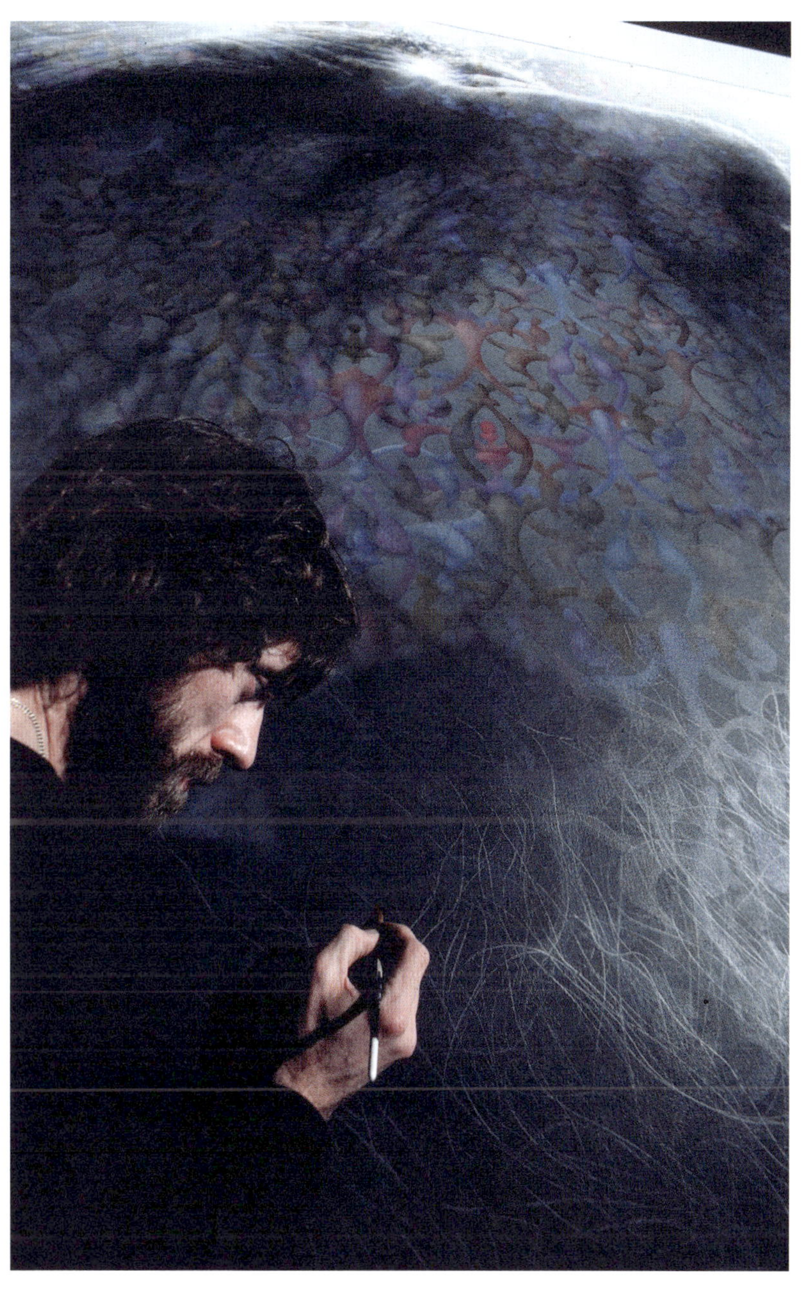

Kaltenbach at work on *Portrait of My Father*, 1970s, Courtesy the artist

SK: During the day. The problem was that I couldn't be there when the museum was closed, and when it was open, there was too much traffic. People wanted to talk to me. I really didn't get much done.

This detail echoes a passage from the life of another singular Bay Area artist, Jay DeFeo, who was at work on her monumental painting, The Rose, *from 1958 to 1966 in her San Francisco apartment. "It was a miracle that I was finally getting to the stage I wanted on the painting — it was practically as good as finished when we got evicted," she said in an interview. Walter Hopps, an enterprising young curator, admirer, and later a friend from Los Angeles, had taken the reins at the Pasadena Art Museum (now the Norton Simon Museum), where he prepared to have the work shipped and publicly presented for the first time.*

On November 9, 1965, all 2,000 pounds of The Rose *was excavated from the artist's second-story window on Fillmore Street by a team of moving men in white jumpsuits. (Bruce Conner made* The White Rose, *an extraordinary film documenting its removal, which included sawing the window open.) DeFeo was in a fragile state of mind in the aftermath of eviction, and in January 1966 followed the work to Pasadena to apply finishing touches; Hopps had installed* The Rose *in a room painted black and used for "desultory storage." DeFeo became ill with the flu, which then spread to just about everyone at the museum. She continued her work on the painting even as she developed dental problems and a palsy, making changes she later noted were important but visible only to herself.*

JS: Tell me about *Crystal Ought*, the gleaming transparent ring that appears on the back cover of the catalogue. The checklist says it's a "study for black velvet painting" from 1979.

SK: I painted that image perhaps five or six times. Because it provided a darker black than black paint, I always worked on velour paper, which had to be sprayed with black acrylic because it faded rather quickly, especially if it got any sun. I considered the *Crystal Ought* to be the image of an immense sculpture made of stars. I also thought of it as an image of the middle letter in the word God.

JS: Much of your thinking was abstract, whereas the paining of Dad was, at least on some important level, a photorealistic portrait of your father. How did it land with the Crocker audience?

SK: I don't know that art always gets the attention that it deserves. To have people share their appreciation blew me away. And now, I'm really grateful that some people do like it enough to tell me that they like it. Really, how fortunate is that? I think it's something that not all artists experience, and I'm grateful.

JS: Why do you think people gravitate toward it?

SK: I'm not completely sure, but there are things that we all have to deal with; either it's in the future, or it has already happened. And these are serious life issues, you know, this painting is an image of where a great deal of my love went for years, and people who talk to me about it, the story is often the same. It's something that helped them in that way. I had, you know, I was going to paint my cat, remember? And there may have been cat lovers who would have liked the cat more, but my experience is that things happen to me, and I do respond. If my sister hadn't sent me that

VOL. 7 NO. 5 Sept./Oct. 1979

a publication of the art guild of the oakland museum association

ART

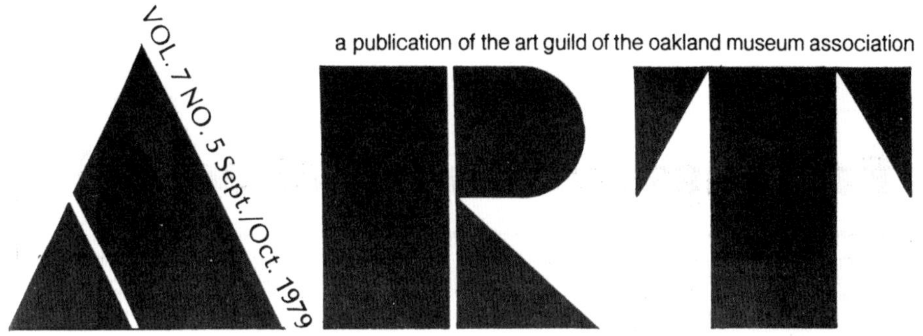

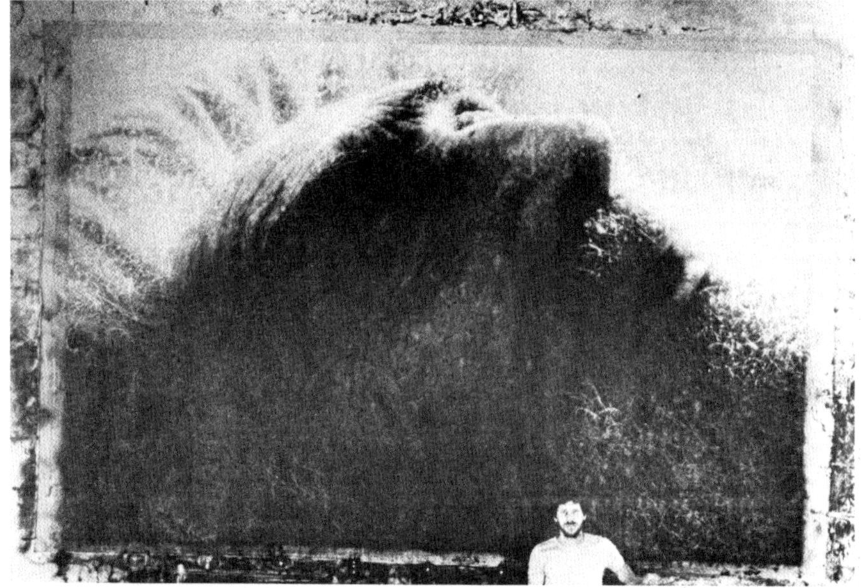

Steven Kaltenbach, *Portrait of My Father,* acrylic on canvas, 114 x 171″, artist in foreground.

ART, September–October 1979, Courtesy Oakland Museum of California

168

photograph, I don't know if you might be looking at a Persian cat, and I can't imagine it having turned out very good.

"… an image of where a great deal of my love went for years." The artist speaking here, the artist addressing life, death, art, and solace: How does he relate to the one arriving to New York 50 years earlier as an upstart craving both esteem and anonymity? One can't help but think that across the arc of his life, Portrait *was the pivot to a more strategy-free embrace of intimacy over esteem, and awe over sophistication. Even in stopping short of explicitly naming death or the passing of parents, he emphasizes that in some critical way the work is out of his hands.*

JS: What happened to the work after it was shown at the Crocker?

SK: When the show ended, the painting returned to my barn. Before long, the Oakland Museum decided they wanted to show it. I think it happened approximately a year later or something.

Portrait of My Father *was displayed at the Oakland Museum of California from October 16 through December 9, 1979, alongside additional material, including astrological charts. Kaltenbach never mentioned the importance of specific dates, times, or relative positions of celestial bodies in our dialogue, but Francesca Wilmott, Curator at the Crocker Art Museum and a Kaltenbach expert, notes that the artist had a vision of the completed painting on December 30, 1974. The Bay Area newsletter* Inside Art *stated in 1979 that the work "was begun on an astrologically propitious day (Dec. 19,*

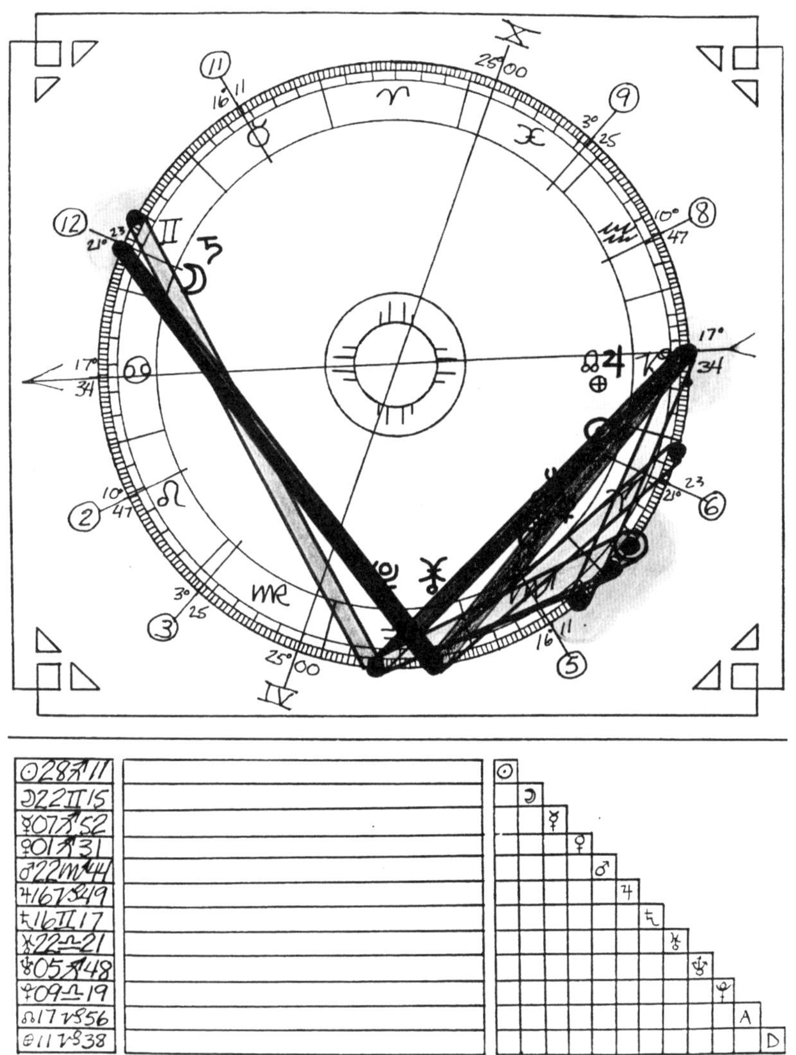

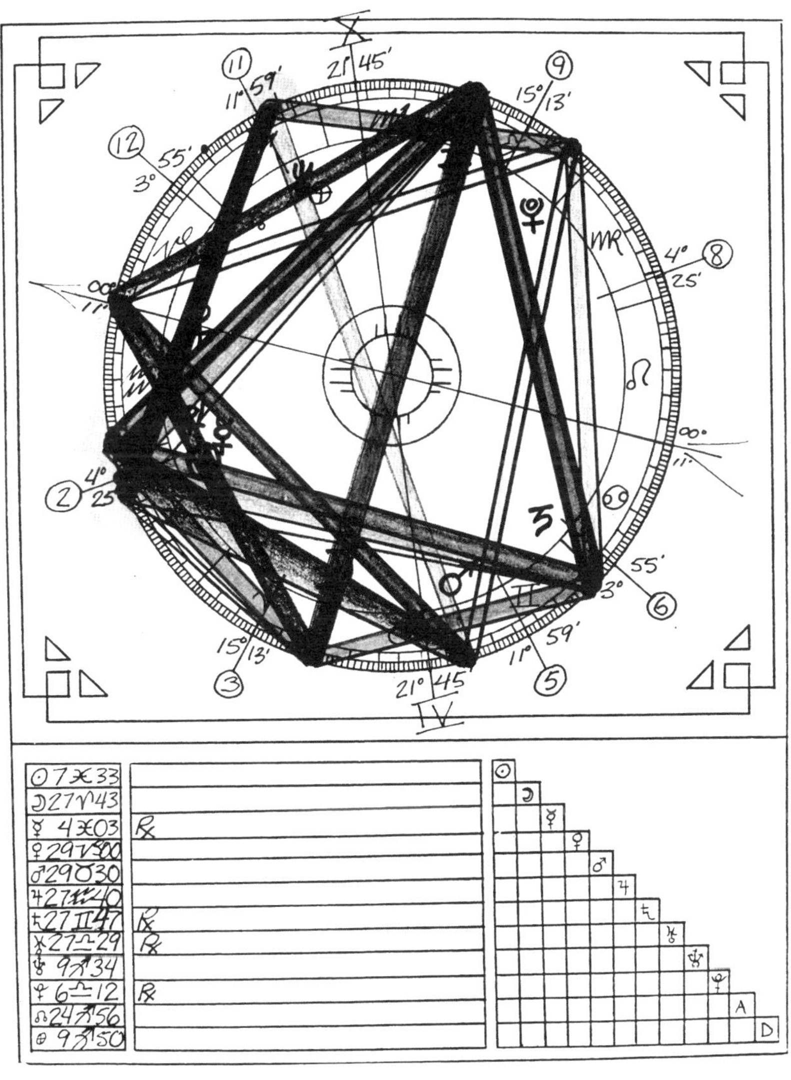

Astrological charts exhibited alongside *Portrait of My Father*, 1970s
Courtesy Crocker Art Museum

1972) with the development of a pattern which would have the properties of a crystal: transparency, solidity and the mystic ability to change color with the light source and surroundings." It also cites the specific time of day at which Kaltenbach photographed his father (November 26, 1973, 7 a.m.) and his first marks on the canvas (February 24, 1974, 5:05 a.m.).

SK: For a long time, I didn't read my reviews. Then I got a really bad review in *The Chronicle*. I think it's probably the worst review I've ever read. It was totally my fault for reading it, but after that I finally felt it was OK to read my reviews because it was entertaining. I'm a little suspicious of approval. It depends. I think if you're strong-minded enough, you can survive it fine, but some people aren't and are affected at least a little bit. Once I gave a talk at the San Francisco Art Institute, and afterward, there was one person who started referring to me as Crazy Kaltenbach. I have to admit that I liked that.

The worst review the artist ever read was printed on October 24, 1979, in the San Francisco Chronicle. *Thomas Albright, respected critic and soon-to-be author of the seminal* Art in the San Francisco Bay Area, 1945–80, *magniloquently wrote: "oh dear, the painting, with its gossamer, neurasthenic, orchid-scented, Neo-Pre-Raphaelite prettiness, is wonderfully corny. But it is not a particularly significant failure, just an inordinately big one" that offers "less and less the more one looks." And in perhaps the worst dig ever leveled at a canvas, Albright compares the work to a Neil Diamond song: "Portrait of My Father is the 'September Morn' of death painting."*

Portrait sits loosely in a kitsch space, with its great big heart on its giant sleeve. But it also wears kitsch as a kind of drag, embodying connection and winning over audiences by using kitsch to get beyond kitsch; while there was plenty on the artist's mind aside from his dying dad, there's not a single viewer who's ever been wrong in their reading or interpretation of the painting, just as he intended. In fact, he made the work specifically for non-art and non-acid-taking audiences, such as his mother.

The painting was stretched in his studio when it returned from Oakland, then rolled up in his office at Sacramento State. It then traveled to the Newport Harbor Museum in Southern California, now the Orange County Museum of Art (OCMA).

SK: I think the most exciting show that happened was in Boulder, Colorado. I had a former student who was working at the Emmanuel Art Gallery and teaching in Boulder; he arranged a show for the *Portrait*. I had a small Toyota pickup. I unstretched the canvas and rolled it around a cardboard tube to keep it from tweaking and folding and messing with the paint, and I drove it out to Colorado. The problem was it was so large that it was sticking out of the pickup four feet out the back.

Former Emmanuel Art Gallery Director Carol Keller notes that she was newly appointed at the time and that Kaltenbach was largely responsible for orchestrating his own show. She was not able to find any surviving records. "Since it was over 40 years ago, I'm short on the details," she wrote in an email.

The Emmanuel Art Gallery is in Denver, not Boulder, and is the city's longest standing religious structure, built in 1876 as a chapel. It is managed by the University of Colorado, Denver.

SK: I didn't leave the barn immediately after the painting was done. I stayed there and continued to work from 1974 to 1982, so it was eight years total. I got married in 1982, and one of the things my fiancée mentioned was that she hoped I didn't have plans for her to move into the barn with me. She made it very clear that was not happening. Strangely enough, my dad was 42 when he married my mom, who was 26. When I got married, I was 42 and I married a woman who was 26. We're still married.

MARY

In the fall of 1978, Mary Flohr, then 22, enrolled in Kaltenbach's advanced painting course as an elective. She was a graduate student in counseling, interested in art therapy and human connection. The class field-tripped to the barn — they'd heard stories about their "famous" professor at work on a huge painting, and he was nearly done with it that season. Mary was awe-struck at the sight of it and attuned to its many paradoxes: "transporting, transparent. So real. Surreal." Captivatingly, she equates her experience of the work with the moment just before sleep, when one reality begins to merge with another.

In Kaltenbach she saw a teacher deeply driven, enchanted with his work and disenchanted with the broader culture, and surprisingly vulnerable in the presence of students. They stayed in touch, and she eventually discovered a man unafraid to share his feelings and engage her in subjects like death and dying, and the ostensible limitlessness of the universe.

Mary is the third of six kids, and had both artists and God in the family, including a priest uncle. She calls her parents excellent and her mother outstanding, emphasizing how they looked after the kids and also how they didn't: their encouragement of wandering and solitude was key to her development.

As she grew, faith became more important than religion, and as her relationship with Kaltenbach flowered, the couple established an unconventional approach to God, praying together not with rote "heavenly father" recitations, but instead with their own unique heart songs. Perhaps most importantly, she saw his ambition, which, tamped down by what she saw as a humility born of a blooming faith, was never stronger than his spirit.

Mary says that when the painting debuted at the Crocker, everyone in her family was there, and proud. She and Kaltenbach stayed in touch, even after she moved to San Diego in pursuit of another degree, and eventually married.

2000

SK: One day a gallery in Sacramento called and said, "We think that the painting should be owned by the Crocker. It should be at the Crocker. That should be its home. We thought we'd check with you and see if you're willing to sell it." I said I would be delighted to have it be cared for at the Crocker. It had been stretched and unstretched so many times that it was getting frayed where it bent over the stretcher at the top. They had to have that repaired, and it's in their collection now.

JS: How did the gallery negotiate the deal with the Crocker?

SK: The two women who ran JAYJAY Gallery were enthused about it. I think they made it reasonable. I believe that the museum decided to see if they could raise money to buy it, and I think that they were able to do that without too much difficulty. I wasn't really paying that much attention, but it seemed as though that wasn't too hard for them to achieve.

> *At the dawn of the new millennium, a pair of Sacramento art dealers, Beth Jones and Linda Jolley, offered* Portrait of My Father *to the Crocker for $75,000. The Crocker is a regional institution, a museum where works on view are united by their connection to a particular place; it's an honest organizing principle and a fitting place for the* Portrait.
>
> *Scott Shields, presently the Associate Director and Chief Curator at the museum, had just begun his now 25-year tenure, and recalls* Portrait *hanging from the rafters of a local church, where it was ceremoniously lowered for his viewing. His encounter provoked "double goose bumps" as the vision slowly sank from the ceiling. (That may have been "W," Kaltenbach's former Sacramento house of worship; neither man can recall.)*
>
> *A sum of $75,000 was significant for a regional museum; it was also a steal given the work's history and gravitas. Intending to raise the money over the course of three years, the Crocker displayed the work as an appeal in itself. In addition to soliciting high-level gifts, they*

installed a clear plastic box beside the painting where they sought to collect cash bills: It was the "Kaltenbox," Shields reports, a direct call for community support. Some measure of modest dollars were stuffed. More consequently, an existing donor who had supported a handful of conservation efforts was especially struck and stepped up with a level of support beyond the terms of the Kaltenbox. Shields says it took only two years to raise the money.

Since the museum's 2010 extension, the painting has hung on a large purpose-built wall. As one might suspect, Portrait of My Father *is an important stop on the official museum tour, and a central work in their collection of more than 25,000 objects. There has been a bench in front of the painting for as long as Shields can remember. "It likes its own wall," he said, adding that elementary school kids eat it up, heaps of them pointing, laughing, and non-chemically tripping out. Reflecting on his prolonged relationship with the work, he says of the painting's subject: "He seemed so very old when I first saw it, but he doesn't seem quite so old as he once did."*

JS: Did you have hopes and dreams for where it might end up in the years before its acquisition? Or anxieties about it not really ending up anywhere? It sounds like you didn't.

SK: Actually, no. Maybe the Pompidou. I'm kidding. I've never been to France. [pause] You just do the work.

The first of three times the painting left the Crocker was for inclusion in Under the Big Black Sun: California Art 1974–81, *a sprawling exhibition curated by Paul Schimmel in 2011 at the Museum of Contemporary Art, Los Angeles, one of more than 60 "Pacific Standard Time" shows throughout the region. The content of Schimmel's exhibition was bookended by Nixon's resignation in 1974 (it included the actual letter) and Reagan's 1981 inauguration, introducing dark, eccentric, and unpredictable social and political realities into what Schimmel understands as the end of Modernism.*

Schimmel was familiar with Kaltenbach's earlier Minimal and Conceptual works and knew of the painting's creation in the barn. While he never saw the work in progress, it was "legendary before it was shown," he said in a phone call.

"No one in LA would ever paint that," Schimmel added, explaining that the animating Northern California spirit of the time was more of a credo: "If you're a really serious artist, then you don't sell out to the market. You don't move to LA." He mentioned other Northern California artists, including Bruce Conner, whose anti-museum stance and distrust of the art world indicated more faith in the possibilities of one's mind than that of the museum. "They all wanted to be outsider artists, which they understood as a desire to remain regional rather than provincial, not part of a bigger, broader scene, not narrow-minded, but rather — and simply — indicative of a particular geographical area."

I saw Portrait of My Father *for the first time at the Berkeley Art Museum and Pacific Film Archive in 2016, when former director Larry Rinder inaugurated his new Diller Scofidio + Renfro building with an eclectic exhibition about the ways in which architecture, when interpreted broadly, "illuminates various aspects of life experience." The painting occupied a considerable part of the northwest gallery wall; facing it at the opening reception stood a gaggle of the confounded.*

"I was floored," Rinder said of first encountering the piece. "Even in my memory it seems so strange and utterly anomalous. One wonders why more art isn't like this, attempting to catch and hold the miracle of life. I guess it's just too hard."

Portrait of My Father *was most recently presented offsite for Kaltenbach's retrospective exhibition in Davis, the one that closed early because of Covid-19 and never reopened.*

Shields reports that while the piece doesn't come off the wall often, there's a trick if it must. Instead of straining to manage its unruly dimensions, art handlers simply lay a soft surface on the floor and let it fall. Portrait of My Father *is so big that the air catches it and it slows itself down, like a room-sized feather.*

SK: I still own almost all my work. I do think it's possible that it'll be valued enough so that people will pay attention to it and collect it. You never know, that kind of thing doesn't always happen. I'm going to be real busy doing all this stuff, and then I'm going to be deceased. I'm going to be enjoying myself in heaven. It's not really going to matter to me very much, although I do have hopes that it will assist my family in having a good, safe life. The challenges of living in this world in the next century are huge. If my family is a little more financially secure, that would maybe be something that would help us. I guess other than things like that, I'm not going to be involved with it.

I just finished reading a book called *The Uninhabitable Earth*, and one of the things that this man [David Wallace-Wells] believes could be the effect of global warming is World War III. In a case like that, we don't even know what would exist afterward. I'm expecting a grandchild in two months, and that child is going to be alive probably in 2100, when they say that our temperature could be up four degrees from what it is.

JS: I hear you saying that there are far greater concerns than your painting. I don't disagree, but do you think about the work's actual, material fate?

SK: Huh. I certainly hope that we keep it together enough so the thing is able to survive and exist. I don't mean to say that the art isn't important to me. I think it is important. It's something that can have important effects on the world, even, and I would like to have positive effects on the world. Also, what can you do? Artists make stuff and sometimes people pay attention to it, and sometimes they pay a lot of attention to it. To me, it's a matter of, *So we'll take what we're doing seriously and do our best, and there it is.*

JS: Do you visit with it?

SK: I'll see it a couple of times a year or something, and it's different every time.

JS: Are you different or is the painting different?

SK: I can't really say. I don't know if it's much of a conceptual experience. There's something, I don't know, comforting about it, to me, that it represents my history, my family tree, you know. It represents a point in time. I got lucky. And we do get lucky. I see it as God's determined path that he wanted me to be on. I'm sorry, but that's how I see it. I'm responsible and I will take credit for … actually, I can't think of anything I can take credit for. I did it, but it all happened to me.

Mary hollers from the background: "You were a conduit!"

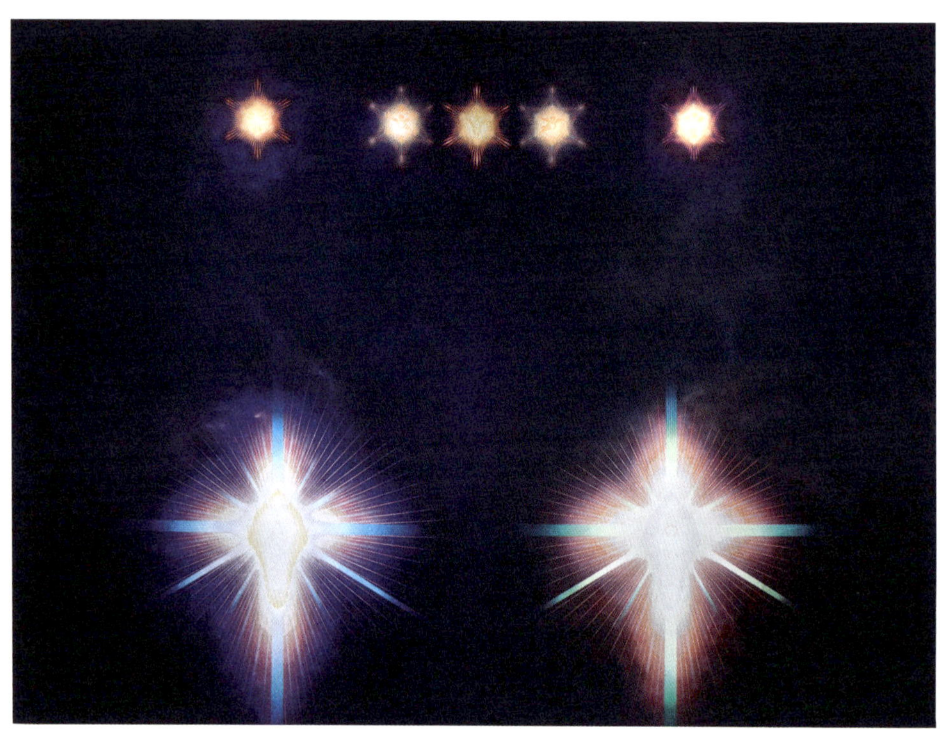

Stephen Kaltenbach, *International Harvester*, 1982-84
Acrylic on canvas, 114 × 147 inches
Collection of the artist, Image courtesy Another Year in LA

Since *Portrait of My Father*, Kaltenbach has more fully embraced a Christian life and religious iconography in his work. In fact, some of his religious paintings hang in one of his former churches. When I asked about them, he seemed sheepish, a little found-out. One is *International Harvester* (1982–84), a 12-foot-wide rendering of a truck blazing through the darkness, illuminated crosses for headlights. That was also made in the barn, though the artist was living elsewhere.

In 2004, he wrote *The End*, a doomsday novel set in a near-future Los Angeles, in which, as the promotional copy indicates, "victims of a series of devastating catastrophes band together in a desperate struggle for survival." It begins: "Mark and Maci were high in more ways than one and for once it wasn't all drug related."

At the same time, he has realized a host of commissioned public art projects in Northern California and beyond, and he's been featured in important group exhibitions, including *State Of Mind: New California Art Circa 1970* (2012–2014), a traveling show curated by Constance Lewallen and Karen Moss; *The Quick and the Dead*, an influential presentation at the Walker Art Center in 2009; Conceptual art reappraisals at the Brooklyn Museum, Hamburger Bahnhof in Berlin, and Museum Morsbroich in Leverkusen, Germany; and *do it*, a roving project curated by Hans Ulrich Obrist featuring instructions from artists that can be used to make art. He has also presented solo exhibitions in commercial contexts like Pierogi, Marlborough Chelsea, Konrad Fischer Galerie, and several at Another Year in LA.

His efforts from the last 55 years are rarely showcased or considered in museum contexts.

When the pandemic slows, I visit with him at home in Davis, where there is religious music on the piano stand — both he and

Mary play — and a curious series of pictures on the wall: several versions of the same artwork, including *Sunset* and *Stone Maple*, photographed at high resolution and printed on canvas via high-quality inkjet reproduction called giclée. There are a few versions of the work at different sizes, and all appear (to some extent) to be painted on. Notably, he does not seem to live with his Conceptual work, and there are no small-scale reproductions of *Portrait of My Father* in the house. The reproductions are not *not* artworks, but it's hard to know what to call them. Perhaps he's borrowing from himself, finding influence and inspiration in recontextualizing his past directly into his present.

The main event in his studio is an in-progress painting of Jesus that Kaltenbach has been focused on for several years, working solely under black light.

Kaltenbach seems relaxed, and if he's pulling anything over on me, as one might expect an earlier version of the artist to do, it's undetectable.

I record the conversation that day, and one quote in particular makes an impression:

> Certainly, we have a right to choose our life path and what we want to do. On the other hand, there's the idea that producing work is like walking across a pond, and you see these works like stepping stones. Some of them are minor and they're below the surface, and they should be at the surface. Some are like air, above the surface, and can't be seen, but deserve to be seen. You can't get to the ones that are the most fulfilling without stepping on the previous stones. You have to go through the whole thing. And now, honestly, really, I am free. It's great as far as I'm concerned. In a way, it's almost something suspect because it's so easy.

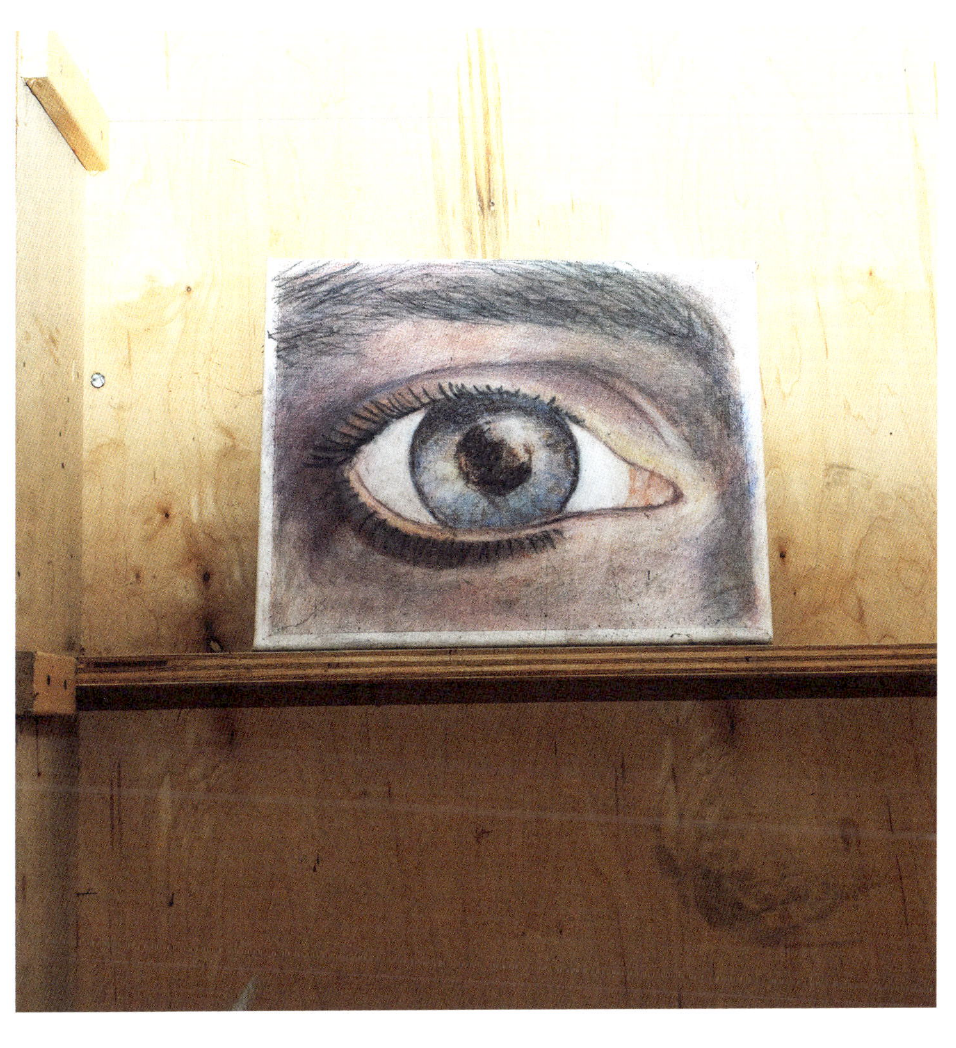

Stephen Kaltenbach, drawing study, ca.2015, Photo: Jason Fulford

One morning Steve calls to tell me he's losing his mind.

"Have I told you I'm getting stupid?" It's his way of letting me know — maybe for the fifth time — that his memory is fading. He wants to communicate something and understands there's a distinct possibility that he may have already told me.

"Well, I've got water aerobics soon, but I wanted to ask you something. Did I ever tell you why the painting is called *Portrait of My Father?*"

"Huh. No. I guess I'd never thought to ask."

"It's because people kept asking me what I was working on, and that's what I would say. That's what it is."

I must have laughed. His "news" is simple, and possibly profound, a familiar feeling in his company. I try to imagine Steve and his fellowship of shallow-enders later that morning: Do they have any idea who their sweet-faced friend is? Do I?

"And did I ever mention what I was going to paint before my dad?"

"Yes, your Persian cat, Teddy."

"Yes, that's right. And did I tell you what I was going to paint after that, after Teddy but before dad?"

"Uh. No. I mean, there was no after-Teddy and before-dad; it was Teddy and then it was dad. That's how you've always explained it."

"Well, ha. Jordan. I was going to paint a 10,000-petal lotus."

Silence.

"It was going to be beautiful."

REFERENCES

Thomas Albright, "A Wonderfully Corny Father," *San Francisco Chronicle*, October 24, 1979.

"'Bad' Painting." New Museum press release, 1978. https://archive.newmuseum.org/exhibitions/5

Roger Clisby and John Fitz Gibbon, *Steven Kaltenbach: Portrait of My Father: A Painting in Progress*. E.B. Crocker Art Gallery, 1979.

John Fitz Gibbon, "Sacramento!" *Art in America* 59 (6), 1971.

Aldous Huxley, *The Doors of Perception*. Harper & Brothers, 1954.

Stephen Kaltenbach, "Artist Statement," Anotheryearinla.com, 2008. https://anotheryearinla.com/Stephen_Kaltenbach_TIME_CAPSULES_Artist_Statement.htm

Stephen Kaltenbach, "Artist Statement," Anotheryearinla.com, 2023. https://www.anotheryearinla.com/2023_StephenKaltenbach.htm

Stephen Kaltenbach, "How to Subvert the Art World and Get Away with It." VICE, May 25, 2016. https://www.vice.com/en/article/stephen-kaltenbach-protocol-of-opposites-essay

Sarah Lehrer-Graiwer, "Stephen Kaltenbach." *Artforum*, September 2010. https://www.artforum.com/columns/stephen-kaltenbach-195219

Sarah Lehrer-Graiwer, *Joint Dialogue*. Overduin and Kite, 2010.

Sarah Lehrer-Graiwer, *Lee Lozano: Dropout Piece*. MIT Press, 2014.

Connie Lewallen and Jordan Stein, "Nothing to Sell: On Reese Palley Gallery." Open Space, March 12, 2020. https://openspace.sfmoma.org/2020/03/nothing-to-sell-on-reese-palley-gallery

Constance Lewallen, Ted Mann, Gwen Allen, Lawrence Rinder, and Sarah Lehre-Graiwer, *Stephen Kaltenbach: The Beginning and the End*. Jan Shrem and Maria Manetti Shrem Museum of Art, 2020.

Lee Lozano, *Lee Lozano: Private Book 5 (89)*. New York: Karma, 2018.

Del McColm. "Kaltenbach's Mystery Painting Shown," *Davis Enterprise–Weekend*, February 16, 1979.

Cindy Nemser, "An Interview with Stephen Kaltenbach."
Artforum, November 1970. https://www.artforum.com/features/
an-interview-with-stephen-kaltenbach-213639

Peter Plagens, "Steve Kaltenbach, Stephen Davis and Howard
Fried." *Artforum*, March 1975. https://www.artforum.com/events/
steve-kaltenbach-stephen-davis-and-howard-fried-232348

William S. Smith, "More Is Less." *ARTnews.com*, December 28, 2020.
https://www.artnews.com/art-in-america/interviews/
barbara-rose-abc-art-1234580339

Jordan Stein, *Rip Tales: Jay DeFeo's Estocada & Other Pieces*. Soberscove
Press, 2021.

Roger White, "The End." In *The Contemporaries: Travels in the 21st-Century Art World*. Bloomsbury, 2015.

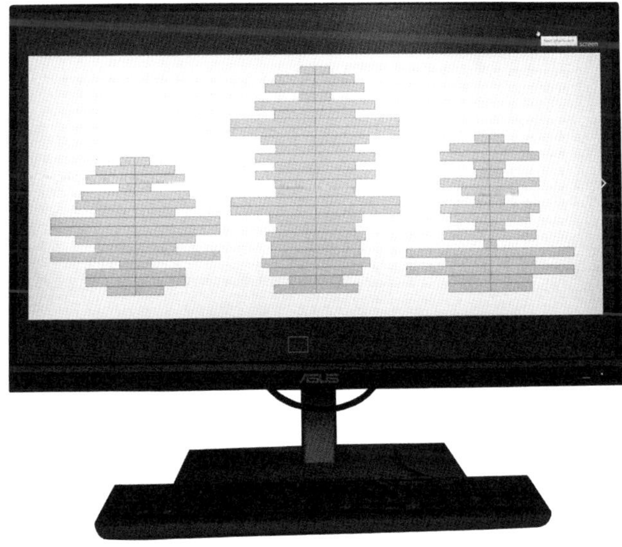

Stephen Kaltenbach, *Gift of Life,* 2024

ACKNOWLEDGEMENTS

This project was supported at the outset by Beth Dungan, a remarkable thinking partner and champion who absolutely made this possible; I can't thank her enough. The book is also supported by The Jenni Crain Foundation, an initiative dedicated to preserving the legacy of the esteemed artist and curator. It's an honor.

Special thanks to Kelly Lindner, Art Galleries and Collections Curator at California State University, Sacramento, for sharing Steve's archives, facilitating their documentation, and catalyzing this project. Thanks also to Francesca Wilmott, PhD, Curator at the Crocker Art Museum, for her invaluable knowledge and support.

For research assistance, I thank David Stone of Another Year in LA; Sophie Fox at *Artforum*; Mariah Briel and Scott Shields from the Crocker Art Museum; Anna Bunting from Oakland Museum of California; David Rozelle at SFMOMA; Róisín Inglesby from William Morris Gallery; Jaap van Liere at the Estate of Lee Lozano; Ted Mann; Tony May; Larry Rinder; and Steve's longtime friend John Torreano, who was particularly generous. Special thanks to Joseph Isaac Cohen, the first reader and shaper of the interview transcriptions, who also provided archival support.

I am indebted to Sarah Lehrer-Graiwer and Roger White for their thoughtful writing on Steve, and to my insightful New York readers, Dan Nadel and Sam Dolnick. Cheers to David DeWitt, a copyeditor who gave a lot of time when he didn't have much of it.

Much appreciation to Claudia La Rocco, a tender, brilliant, and exacting editor. I'm grateful for our ongoing dialogue. Sincere thanks to Jason Fulford — artist, designer, publisher, friend, and J&L Books factotum — who enthusiastically supported this project with both talent and patience. I suppose it helped that both our fathers are Steves (mine Stephen, his Steven). Lindsey White remains my guiding light. Thank you.

Heartfelt thanks to Mary Kaltenbach for her grace and participation. Most importantly, my gratitude to Steve, an inspiration and mystery of the highest order. They don't make 'em like you anymore.

Front cover:
Stephen Kaltenbach, *Portrait of My Father* (detail)

Front flap:
Steven Kaltenbach holding the remnants of the Plexglas "still life" in
Sacramento, CA, 2025. Photo: Jason Fulford

Inside front flap:
Stephen Kaltenbach, *Portrait of My Father*, 1972-79
Acrylic on canvas, 114 × 170 inches
Crocker Art Museum Purchase with contributions from Gerald D. Cordon,
Collectors' Guild, Anne and Malcolm McHenry, Kim Mueller and Robert J.
Slobe, James R. Lenarz and other donations, 2001.85

Back cover:
Steven Kaltenbach and *Portrait of My Father* in the barn, ca.1979
Courtesy the artist

Back flap:
The Sacrmento Union, March 1, 1979

Inside back flap:
(all) Courtesy Crocker Art Museum